CONTENTS

ILLUSTRATIONS

Notes to the pictures, additional to the captions, are given here when necessary

1a A Viking ship, reconstructed. *From the Oslo Museum*

A replica crossed the Atlantic in 1893. (See N. Nicolaysen, *The Viking-Ship discovered at Gokstad*, Oslo, 1882; T. D. Kendrick, *History of the Vikings*, London, 1930, pp. 24 f.).

1b Ornamental purse-lid. *From Sutton Hoo Ship Burial, British Museum*

The lid itself has perished: it was probably of bone or ivory; the hinges, frame and plaques survive. The hexagonal plaques are the most elaborate examples of the cloisonné work characteristic of the Sutton Hoo jewellery. In the centre are two birds of prey capturing ducks; on either side is a man between two animals, possibly Daniel in the lion's den.

2 Offa's dyke on Llanvair Hill, Shropshire. *From a photograph by Dr. J. K. S. St. Joseph (Crown Copyright reserved)*

This view shows the dyke running south-east over the hill; as it descends it turns and follows what is now a line of trees: at the turn the surveyors of the dyke aligned it on Cwmsanaham Hill opposite (just out of view): in 1½ miles it never deviates more than 50 yards from this line (see Sir Cyril Fox, *Offa's Dyke*, London, 1955, p. 136).

3a–c "Standard", helmet and whetstone. *From the Sutton Hoo Ship Burial, British Museum* (See page 203)

The helmet is of iron, with gilt- and tinned-bronze and silver plaques attached. One of the plaques is virtually identical with a tiny fragment of a helmet found in the royal burial ground at Gama Uppsala in Sweden, and so the helmet is generally thought to have come from Sweden. The other two objects have been supposed to be a royal standard and a ceremonial whetstone, a kind of sceptre, symbol of the king as Wayland the Smith, the master of swords. But this may be wrong, and the standard has been variously interpreted as a lamp-stand, on which torches of pine-chips could be put to light the high table in the hall, and as a scalp-rack (see page 53).

3d A Saxon cathedral: North Elmham, Norfolk. *From a photograph by Dr. J. K. S. St. Joseph (Crown Copyright reserved)*

4a A passage from Beowulf. *From British Museum, Cotton MS. Vitellius A. xv, f. 130v (c. 1000)*

The manuscript was damaged in the Cotton fire in 1731. As time passed the charred edges fell off, but before this happened copies had been made from which we can reconstruct the missing words.

4b Domesday Book: a passage from the first page of Wiltshire enlarged (vol. I, f.64v). *Crown Copyright, reproduced by permission of the Controller of H.M. Stationery Office*

ILLUSTRATIONS

5a The king in majesty, with orb and sceptre: coin of Edward Confessor. *From the Ashmolean Museum*

This and the seal show clear "imperial" influence: the coin, of the Byzantine empire, since it is an imitation of a coin of Justinian's cousin and successor, Justin II; the seal, of the German empire, since the obverse is a close copy of the imperial seals of the eleventh century (see R. H. M. Dolley and F. E. Jones in *Anglo-Saxon Coins*, ed. Dolley, London, 1961, pp. 215 ff.).

5b Edward the Confessor: forged seal. *From the British Museum*

The matrix from which these impressions, obverse and reverse, were taken, was made by a forger of genius working at Westminster Abbey in the mid-twelfth century. His seals were used for forged charters of a number of religious houses. This seal is a close copy of the genuine seal of the Confessor, the oldest version of the great seal known, but the genuine specimens are not sufficiently well preserved to reproduce here.

5c William II: genuine seal, reverse. *From the British Museum*

A cast from a Durham charter. (On figures 5b and 5c see W. de G. Birch, *Catalogue of Seals in the British Museum*, I, London, 1887, nos. 5, 7, 22; T. A. M. Bishop and P. Chaplais, *Facsimiles of English Royal Writs to 1100*, Oxford, 1957, pp. xix ff., and for the genuine seal of the Confessor and the original of figure 5c, plates xviii, viii.)

6a King Athelstan presents a book to St. Cuthbert. *From Corpus Christi College, Cambridge, MS. 183, f.1v*

(See R. A. B. Mynors, *Durham Cathedral Manuscripts*, Oxford, 1939, p. 26; B. Colgrave, *Two Lives of St. Cuthbert*, Cambridge, 1940, esp. pp. 20-1.)

6b A Saxon fortified town: Wallingford, Berkshire. *From a photograph by Dr. J. K. S. St. Joseph (Crown Copyright reserved)*

The line of fortifications at the top is broken by the Norman castle, whose remains are in the top right-hand corner, covering the bridge. Wallingford was the key fortress in the warfare between Stephen and the future Henry II in 1153: Stephen, besieging the town, faced Henry, trying to relieve it from the other side of the river; but a truce was made before they joined battle. (On Wallingford, see M. W. Beresford and J. K. S. St. Joseph, *Medieval England*, Cambridge, 1958, pp. 179-81.)

7a King Cnut and Queen Emma (Ælfgyfu) present a gift to the New Minster, Winchester. *From British Museum, Stowe MS. 944, f.6.*

The queen's veil and the king's crown are held by angels, who point a finger at Christ, the source of royal power. A fine example of late pre-Conquest drawing (1020-30: F. Wormald, *English Drawings of the tenth and eleventh centuries*, London, 1952, pp. 72-3).

7b On his return from Normandy, Harold visits Edward the Confessor. *From the Bayeux Tapestry*

8a, e Gold rings of Æthelswyth, queen of Mercia (855-88) and Æthelwulf, king of Wessex (839-58). *From the British Museum*

These were Alfred's sister and father. The rings are inscribed "Eathelswith regina" and "Etheluulf rex"; the queen's ring has on it the lamb of God.

8b,c,d, The Alfred Jewel. *From the Ashmolean Museum*

This delightful piece of jewellery, 2½ inches long, is made of gold with an enamel portrait under crystal. It was found near Athelney in the seventeenth century, and there is no reason to doubt that it was made for King Alfred. It has been suggested that the figure is a king holding a sceptre in each hand (see Schramm, *Herrschaftszeichen*, I, 370-5; and Joan R. Clarke, *The Alfred and Minster Lovel Jewels*, Oxford, 2nd Edn., 1961).

ILLUSTRATIONS

9a-e Anglo-Saxon Coins. *From the Ashmolean Museum (see G. C. Brooke, English Coins, rev. edn., London, 1950: Anglo-Saxon Coins, ed. R. H. M. Dolley, London, 1961)*

Ethelred the Unready
Cnut, with a helmet
Edward the Confessor, c. 1053-6
Edward the Confessor, 1065-6
Harold II, 1066

9f The death of Edward the Confessor. *From the Bayeux Tapestry*

Edward's death is the centre of a long tableau: to its left he is being carried to Westminster Abbey for burial: to its right the crown is given to Harold, and beyond is Harold's coronation (see 10a). Why is the story twisted out of order in this way, so that the king appears to be buried before he dies? Partly, it seems, to indicate the speed with which Harold succeeded; partly, so as not to divide the king's deathbed from the presentation of the crown to Harold. The man who offers Harold the crown points at the double scene, at the king's dying speech and his death. (See page 30.)

10a The coronation of Harold. *From the Bayeux Tapestry*

Three stages of the coronation service have been fitted into this scene. On the right the archbishop calls on the people to acclaim (the *collaudatio*—or perhaps he is summoning them to do homage); on the left the sword is presented to him; in the centre he sits enthroned and crowned (see page 34). The archbishop is not shown crowning Harold: this may have been done by the archbishop of York, because Stigand was under a cloud. But if so, the Tapestry is guilty of cunning propaganda, since anyone would assume that the archbishop who performed the *collaudatio* (or summoned to homage) performed the rest of the rite.

10b The death of Harold. *From the Bayeux Tapestry*

This picture is a riddle. An early tradition has it that Harold was killed by an arrow in his eye, so it was long assumed that he was the third figure from the left, the largest figure in the group. But the scene culminates in the dramatic slaughter of another figure. Which is Harold? Or do both figures represent him—just as William is twice represented as the Norman army marches out of Hastings? (It should be noted that the end of the Tapestry was much restored in the nineteenth century)

11a The Norman camp at Hastings is fortified. *From the Bayeux Tapestry*

An officer supervises the building of a castle, a mound or motte with a wooden tower on its summit.

11b The "White Tower", keep of the Tower of London. *Crown Copyright, reproduced by permission of the Ministry of Public Building and Works*

12 The four Norman Kings, by Matthew Paris, c. 1250. *From the British Museum, Royal MS. 14.C.vii, f.8v*

These pictures by the famous monk of St. Albans, historian and artist, Matthew Paris, are not in the modern sense portraits, but they are the source of numerous modern pictures of the kings, from seventeenth-century engravings to twentieth-century cigarette cards. (On Matthew, see R. Vaughan, *Matthew Paris*, Cambridge, 1959, esp. p. 231)

Map of the English Kingdoms, p. 85

Map of the Norman Empire, p. 147

PREFACE

One cannot write biographies, in the usual sense of the word, of Saxon and Norman kings, and there are no portraits of them to show us at all clearly what they looked like. This book was therefore bound to be different in its aim from those on the kings in modern centuries. I hope I have made clear in the introduction what is attempted; to which must be added that although there are a number of pictures of kings among the illustrations, not one was meant to be a portrait in the modern sense. They are, I hope, none the less interesting. But inevitably they need more explanation than a collection of portraits, and fairly full notes have been provided, distributed between the *List of Illustrations* and the captions.

The text is a rendering, *tel quel*, of some of what I have learned over the years from pupils, friends and teachers. A few of my many debts must be specially noted. What I owe to Mr. H. E. Walker cannot be easily summarised: what I say about the origins of Wessex (see pages 199-200) and the *Bayeux Tapestry* draws heavily on his suggestions and insight. My wife and Dr. H. Mayr-Harting read the whole book in manuscript, and the latter has also read it in proof; both have suggested improvements and eradicated many errors and infelicities, though they are not to be reproached for those which remain. I have also had generous help and advice from Dr. P. Chaplais, Mr. J. V. H. Eames, Professor M. Gluckman, Mr. P. Hunter Blair, Dr. E. Peters, Mr. A. Thompson and from the publishers.

I am very grateful to the following for granting permission for extracts to be quoted: to Mrs. Marjorie Chibnall and Messrs. T. Nelson and Sons Ltd., for the extracts from John of Salisbury's *Historia Pontificalis*; to Professor Dorothy Whitelock, and Messrs. Eyre and Spottiswoode Ltd., for the extracts from *English Historical Documents*, vol. 1; to Professor F. Barlow and Messrs. Nelson for the extracts from

The Life of King Edward the Confessor; to Dr. Margaret Murray and Messrs. Faber and Faber for the extracts from *God of the Witches*; to Professor G. N. Garmonsway and Messrs. J. M. Dent and Sons Ltd., for the extracts from the *Anglo-Saxon Chronicle* (Everyman's Library); to Dom Thomas Symons and Messrs. Nelson for the extract from the *Regularis Concordia*; to Mr. D. Wright and Penguin Books Ltd., for the extracts from *Beowulf* (for full references, see pages 196 ff.). Special thanks are also due to the Phaidon Press Ltd., for permission to reproduce photographs from *The Bayeux Tapestry*, edited by Sir Frank Stenton; acknowledgement for the other illustrations is made in the *List of Illustrations*.

H. R. Loyn, *Anglo-Saxon England and the Norman Conquest*, which contains a number of aperçus on English kingship, and J. M. Wallace-Hadrill, *The Long-haired kings and other studies in Frankish history* (both London, 1962) appeared too late to guide me before this book was written, although I had had the benefit of hearing and discussing with Mr. Wallace-Hadrill a part of the new essays in his book.

(1962)   C.N.L.B.

The opportunity of reprints has been taken to correct misprints and minor errors; for help with these I am particularly indebted to Mr. R. H. M. Dolley, Mr. C. A. H. Franklyn, Professor Dom David Knowles, Professor Peter Sawyer and the late Mr. Harold Walker. More than slight correction is not possible at this stage, but a short note on recent literature and on new views on Sutton Hoo and on the events of 1066 has been added on page 203.

November, 1964; October, 1965; October, 1971   C.N.L.B.

CHAPTER I

THE METHOD OF THIS INQUIRY

The further back we go from the modern world into the Middle Ages, the less material the historian has to work on. If a man wishes to study human society at work in detail, or to learn how to select the significant details from a mass of information, he will do better to study very recent history. If he wishes to understand and enjoy the detective element in history, to see how one can wring information from a few scattered clues—or if he wishes to see human nature at work in a different context from his own, to stir his imagination by studying his own remote ancestors, remote not only in time but in their thoughts and interests—then he will be well advised to study the Middle Ages, and will be richly rewarded for his efforts. This book could not hope to be a collection of biographies, like others in the series: the kings were too many; our information is too sparse. I have therefore, quite deliberately, made it a collection of problems: how were kings made? What did they do? How did we come to have kings at all? In the earlier chapters, by pursuing these questions, I hope to elucidate the nature of early kingship, to free it from the strange political notions which are inclined to cling to it, sometimes because of modern preconceptions, sometimes because of the lingering influence of seventeenth- or nineteenth-century historians, who saw in kingship the origins of seventeenth-century tyranny, and in royal councils the origins of parliamentary liberty.

We shall find that early kingship was surrounded by very different ideas from those to which we are accustomed; and as we pursue the story of the early English kings we shall see some of these ideas working out in practice. The early kings are rarely more than names; but as the centuries pass we find some who left their mark on English history—Ethelbert, Edwin, Offa—and from the time of Alfred (871-99) on we know something more of all the English kings than their dates and their battles. By whatever route the sources open to us I have tried to pursue these kings and reveal what manner of men they were—their tastes and interests and achievements. It is by worrying over some particular problem that we can hope best to get to know them. Why was King Athelstan so great a connoisseur of " relics "? Was William II a religious sceptic? Was Henry I an accessory to the murder of William II? One major difficulty is that we rarely know the physical appearance of these men. No portraits, in the modern sense, survive of any of them. We have some sort of description of Edward the Confessor and the first three Norman kings; we have " pictures " of many kings—but they are all stylised and conventional. None the less the trappings of kingship, crowns, armour, costume, palaces, castles, and other objects more or less intimately connected with them— rings and jewels made for them, books written for them, coins struck in their name—can give us some kind of physical contact with them; and in the Bayeux Tapestry we see the story of the Norman Conquest told by an English artist for the benefit of one of the greatest of Norman lords, Odo, bishop of Bayeux, the Conqueror's half-brother. In it are shown Edward the Confessor and Harold as well as William the Conqueror. From all these sources the illustrations are drawn: they are an essential part of our purpose, which is to find out what we can know of the Saxon and Norman kings of England.[1]

It is sometimes thought that the real pursuit of historical problems cannot be undertaken without a heavy panoply of footnotes and technical arguments. There is, of course, a great deal of truth in this, and it has been one of the chief difficulties in writing this book to make the arguments genuine without making them too technical. In part I have evaded this by relegating all detailed references to an appendix,

[1] I have deliberately made no attempt to include the kings of Wales and Scotland: their story is no less interesting, but it is quite different, and cannot be treated as an appendix to English history.

which I hope is adequate to show serious students the materials on which the text is based. But I have also been aware that if we remove the element of quest, the pursuit of problems, the " burrowing into wormholes ", we remove from history a great part of its interest. The study of medieval history, especially of the early Middle Ages, is largely detective work, and there is no reason why it should not be widely enjoyed as such.

My theme is English kingship: kingship as it was known to the Germanic people, the Anglo-Saxons, who conquered and settled what we call " England " in the fifth and sixth centuries; who formed a multiplicity of tiny kingdoms, out of which the kingship of England grew. The period stretches roughly from 450 to 1154. In 400 most of the island had been part of the Roman empire; in 406 the Vandals and the Burgundians broke across the Rhine into Gaul; in 410 Alaric and the Visigoths sacked Rome itself. The Roman empire in the east survived until 1453; the Roman empire in the west died in the fifth century—died in fact, that is, for its memory lingered on, a potent influence on all its former provinces. Meanwhile military disaster led the Romans to abandon Britain, and leave it a prey to barbarian attackers—from Ireland (the " Scots "), from Scotland (the " Picts ") and from Germany. The Roman provinces were broken up into kingdoms, whose precise number and extent are quite unknown. Tradition has it that the greatest of these was ruled by a king called Vortigern in the mid-fifth century. We know that Saxons from northern Germany had visited England as pirates and mercenaries for some generations before the time of Vortigern; but Vortigern is said to have raised an especially powerful force of Saxon mercenaries under leaders called Hengest and Horsa. The Saxons presently turned on their master, and formed a kingdom of their own, traditionally supposed to be the kingdom of Kent. From then on settlers from northern Germany came in numerous shiploads, sailed up the Thames, the rivers of the Wash and Humber, settled, formed little kingdoms and confederations, and conquered the native " Britons ". The Britons were not wholly defenceless.

Early in the sixth century they found a great leader, whom tradition calls Arthur, who drove the German invaders out of a great part of the south midlands. But this success was not lasting. By the late sixth century the Germans had recovered what they had lost; they had conquered at least two-thirds of what we call England, and their supremacy was rapidly admitted in the rest.

The invaders are commonly called the Angles, Saxons and Jutes. The Saxons came from northern Germany (" Old Saxony", what we should call north-western Germany), the Angles from where Germany and Denmark meet, the Jutes (to cut a long story short) most probably from Friesland or the Rhineland. In England they met and mingled; very roughly, the Angles preponderated in the north and midlands, the Saxons in the south and west, the Jutes in Kent and Hampshire. By 600 the country was firmly settled by the " Anglo-Saxons ", and a group of leading kingdoms was beginning to emerge: the chief were Northumbria, the most powerful kingdom of the seventh century, Mercia, which, after challenging Northumbria in the seventh century, won supremacy in its turn in the eighth, and Wessex, which after a late start emerged the leader in the early ninth century. Also about 600 took place the central event of Anglo-Saxon history, the mission of St. Augustine from Rome to begin the conversion of the English. In the decades following 597 missionaries both from Rome and from Christian Ireland, Wales and Scotland worked with great effort among the pagan Anglo-Saxons. In the late seventh century the English Church was firmly organised by a Syrian Greek, sent at an advanced age by the pope to be archbishop of Canterbury, Theodore of Tarsus. By that time most of the English kingdoms were Christian, at least in name; and in the eighth century, in the days of the Venerable Bede, the English Church was one of the centres of western civilisation.

In the early ninth century Wessex became supreme; by the end of the ninth century it was the only English kingdom; in the tenth and eleventh centuries it was converted into the kingdom of England. This was the joint work of the Danish invaders and the dynasty of King Alfred. The Danes raided, and then settled in England in the ninth century; by 871 they had conquered most of it, Wessex excepted. The other royal dynasties became extinct. From 871 to 899 England was ruled by Alfred, an indefatigable warrior, and a man who showed exceptional imagination in the arts both of peace and of war. He just saved Wessex, and laid foundations on which his successors were able to build a united English kingdom; but this could hardly have happened if he had not been succeeded by a line of notably able rulers, his son Edward the Elder (899-925), his grandson Athelstan (925-39) and his great-grandson Edgar (959-75) in particular. The Danes were pagan, and the conversion of England had, in some measure, to start again. This was rapidly accomplished in the wake of the ecclesiastical revival of the tenth century, a movement of reform, particularly of monastic reform. The revival of English kingship, however, was rudely checked at the end of the tenth century, when Danish attacks began once again. In 1013 the Danish Swein completed the process of dispossessing the English Ethelred the " Unready "; but in 1014 Swein died, and it was not until 1016 that his younger son, Cnut, was firmly established as king. Cnut could command the loyalty of both his English and Danish subjects in equal measure, and so, in a special sense, was first king of the united kingdom of England.

Cnut died young; and soon after his death the kingdom reverted to the native English line in the person of Edward the Confessor (1042-66). Edward's death in 1066 was the signal for the most famous crisis in English history. He was succeeded by his brother-in-law Harold II; but nine months later Harold fell under a Norman arrow or a Norman axe at Hastings, and the Normans ruled in his stead. The period closes with the reigns of William the Conqueror (1066-87), his two sons, William II (1087-1100) and Henry I (1100-35), and his grandson, Henry's nephew, Stephen (1135-54).

Of all these kings Alfred is the one about whom we are best informed. We have a number of works written or inspired by himself—his translations and his laws; we have

Asser's *Life*. This is not a masterpiece of biography, and its authenticity has been seriously questioned. The dispute continues, but must for the present be ignored. Asser's *Life* is a sandwich, made up of a version of the *Anglo-Saxon Chronicle*, with a description of various aspects of Alfred's life and activity squeezed into it; in this book I have assumed that the latter can reasonably be used as evidence of what a well-informed but not over-intelligent contemporary resident in Alfred's court thought to be true. This is still the view held by most scholars—though it may yet have to be abandoned.

Alfred is the only king whose own writings survive from this period; and one of the very few who were literate. Of early kings we have vignettes and other valuable information in the pages of Bede's splendid *Ecclesiastical History* (731), the finest historical work produced by any scholar in Europe in this period. Of later kings we have accounts in a variety of chronicles and other narrative sources; of Edward the Confessor we have a contemporary biography; of the Norman kings we have panegyrics and chronicles of various kinds. Of most Saxon kings before Alfred, and many after, we have no narrative account, beyond the brief annals in the *Anglo-Saxon Chronicle*. Of the kings of the lesser kingdoms, we usually know little but their names; of the kings of Lindsey we know nothing but their names; the kings of the Middle Angles and the Middle Saxons (if kings they had) are wholly anonymous.

The early kings, save those fortunate enough to find a place in Bede, must be pursued through one of four channels; the *Anglo-Saxon Chronicle*, genealogies, vernacular poetry, archaeology. The *Chronicle*, as we know it, was drawn up in the reign of Alfred; it was a part of that renaissance of which the king was centre, which produced works in the vernacular, rather than in the normal language of literature, Latin, because the king wished them to be understood by a wider circle. Whether Alfred himself inspired the *Chronicle* is disputed; but it is difficult not to see in it the reflection of his interests, or to doubt that he perused a copy of it. One of the copies made in his lifetime is still preserved in the library of

Corpus Christi College, Cambridge. From this and from later copies which were distributed and continued at various monasteries, we have versions of the chronicle down to the Norman Conquest and even a little beyond; one version was continued, first at Canterbury, then at Peterborough, down to 1154, and gives towards the end a famous description of the reign of King Stephen.

Sources of the Norman period are much more prolific than those of the Saxon, especially of the early Saxon. This is not mainly due to the chance of survival—though countless medieval manuscripts, of course, have disappeared. Mainly it is because far less was written in the seventh century, or in the ninth, than in the twelfth. Even comparatively literate ages, like the age of Bede or of Dunstan (died 988), produced far less than the age of the " twelfth-century renaissance ". Of this little, a remarkable proportion has survived. The Bodleian library at Oxford contains a copy of one of King Alfred's translations sent by himself to Worcester Cathedral; the Corpus library contains a ninth-century manuscript of the *Chronicle*, and a book which King Athelstan in person gave to the community of St. Cuthbert, then at Chester-le-Street (later of Durham Cathedral) (*figure 6a*); the Cotton collection in the British Museum contains two of the five surviving copies of Bede's *History*, which were written in Bede's own century, before 800. It is no chance that we find these books in Cotton's collection or in Corpus. After the Dissolution of the monasteries, most medieval manuscripts tended to be destroyed; the invention of printing had made many of them seem valueless. But there were men in the sixteenth century like Matthew Parker, archbishop of Canterbury under Elizabeth I, who were passionately interested in the early history of the English Church—a natural interest in the wake of the Reformation. Parker and his secretaries were fanatical collectors of early manuscripts, especially of early chronicles; and Parker's collection was left to Corpus Christi College, Cambridge, of which he had once been Master. A little later there appeared a collector of equal avidity in Sir

Robert Cotton, who shared Parker's interest in the Church; but was also much concerned with developing theories of parliamentary origins. It was widely thought in the early seventeenth century that our parliamentary liberties were derived from the Anglo-Saxon Witan; and this gave Cotton a special interest in Saxon charters, whose long lists of signatories or witnesses are almost our only information on who formed the "Witan". It is probably true to say that the majority of pre-Conquest original charters owe their survival to Sir Robert Cotton. The practical concerns (not to say fantasies) of Parker and Cotton, coupled with a genuine devotion to the past, saved much valuable evidence in the nick of time. For this we must be grateful to them; but, for the earlier Saxon period, there was mighty little to save.

The Parker copy of the *Chronicle*, Asser's *Life* (the manuscript of which was preserved by Cotton, but burnt in the disastrous fire of 1731 and so is only known from sixteenth- and seventeenth-century copies), Athelstan's gift to St. Cuthbert (*figure 6a*), and other manuscripts—including one of the early ninth century in Cotton's collection—contain genealogies and lists of early English kings. From these, if treated with a certain measure of scepticism, and checked wherever possible by other evidence, we can reconstruct lists of early dynasties. It is not perhaps an inspiring thought that we ourselves might be represented to future generations by something akin to a telephone directory; but skilful probing has enabled the experts to derive much interesting information from these lists and genealogies. And the survival of early poetry, especially of the splendid epic *Beowulf*—another of Sir Robert Cotton's finds—enables us to put a little flesh on the dry bones.

Beowulf also helps us to clothe the kings and imagine the houses they lived in; and it has in these respects been marvellously supplemented in recent years by archaeology. The spade has unearthed many relics of this period: from graves, from settlements, from Saxon and Norman churches and towns, and Norman castles. But the archaeologist can only dig up what is lasting; that is, broadly speaking, stone and pottery, metal which rust has not wholly corrupted, and bones; but not wood or cloth. It is therefore somewhat ironical that the most sensational finds of Saxon archaeology have been the wooden ship at Sutton Hoo and the timber halls of the palace at Yeavering. At Sutton Hoo the timber had rotted, but the iron bolts were still visible, and the marks of the timbers could still be traced in the soil; and in any case it was the contents of the boat which made the discovery so exciting. At Yeavering the timber had entirely disappeared. But timber halls are built round posts set in postholes, or by driving a row of timbers into slots. When the timber rots, the holes are filled in with soil from the surface, of a different quality from that surrounding the hole. This affects the fertility of the area of the hole, so that when the soil is richer corn grown to-day will be higher, when less rich, lower, than over the rest of the surrounding ground. Normally this would be extremely difficult to observe. But from an aeroplane, flying low over the field in early dawn or late evening, when the sun is low, one can see the shadow cast by the higher crops on the lower; and so an aerial photograph taken under these conditions will reveal the pattern of a timber hall centuries after the timber has completely disappeared. Thus was Yeavering discovered; and the palace of the Northumbrian kings has since been excavated.

Later in the period the sources become more diverse: a regular currency provides the archaeologist with large finds of coins; growing literacy provides the historian with a mass of charters, laws and (by the eleventh and twelfth centuries) chronicles and biographies to read; more stone buildings—especially the tremendous buildings thrown up in such numbers by the early Normans—give us more substantial, visible monuments of the past; and the chance survival of a remarkable piece of embroidery gives us in the Bayeux Tapestry a chronicle and a film-strip combined: we can study events, and armour and costume, and many other things, all at once.

This is not meant to be a catalogue, and is far from complete. As we proceed, I shall try to reveal from time to time how historians use these various materials to reconstruct the past; and explain some in more detail, and introduce others not here described. In this period it is often more interesting, more exciting, more intellectually satisfying, to consider how we know rather than what we know.

CHAPTER II

ON KING-MAKING

In Prof. Plumb's *The First Four Georges* we are introduced to four kings spanning a little more than a hundred years. The assignment of this book is seven hundred years and perhaps two hundred kings. Worse still, the large majority of them are so obscure we know only their names; a few are wholly anonymous. Yet the study of these distant figures has a special fascination: their obscurity challenges us to find every clue and follow it wherever it leads us; and if we do this we shall find that we can learn a surprising amount about the early English kings. We shall also find ourselves inspecting the roots of English kingship, of our oldest and most characteristic institution of government; and that too is rewarding It will help us to understand some things about English monarchy, some of the reasons why its continuity has been so little broken; but it will only do this if we are quite clear at the outset that in most particulars the kingship of Saxon and Norman times was utterly unlike the constitutional monarchy of Elizabeth II.

Historical labels easily deceive us, and some of the most deceptive are those which surround ideas of government and kingship. Nobody imagines that a medieval king, whether of England, France or Germany, was a constitutional monarch in the modern sense. But one often hears or reads discussions on whether they were limited or absolute, elective or hereditary. No doubt we shall keep these problems in the back of our minds as we study these kings and the manner of their rule, but in the front of our minds we should be concerned with less abstract notions. If we observe how men acted and how they described their actions we shall get a much sharper focus on their assumptions; we shall see their minds more as the human mind really is, not as the mirror of coherent principles of political thought, but as the battlefield of conflicting assumptions and aspirations, without evident coherence. Human nature, the psychologists tell us, is liable to change. But the nobleman who acclaimed a Saxon king was acting on a mingling of impulses as rich, confused and intriguing as a modern voter. This is not to underestimate the interest of political theory or its influence on human affairs; as we shall see, intellectual influences utterly remote from the native tradition of the Saxon peoples played a crucial part in moulding English monarchy. But the meaning of this will only become clear as we inspect some of the peculiarities of early kingship; and the first problem is to try to discover how kings were made.

This problem has been the subject of many extraordinary notions. In 1867, in the first volume of his great *History of the Norman Conquest of England*, Edward Augustus Freeman propounded one of the most preposterous. In writing of the Witenagemot, the Anglo-Saxon royal council, he said: " In one sense it was more democratic than anything that the most advanced Liberal would venture to dream of; in another sense it was more oligarchic than anything that the most unbending Conservative would venture to defend. Yet it may in practice have fairly represented the wishes of the nation; and, if so, no people ever enjoyed more complete political freedom than the English did in these early times. For the powers of the ancient Witenagemot surpassed beyond all measure the powers which our written Law vests in a modern Parliament. In some respects they surpassed the powers which our conventional Constitution vests in the House of Commons. The King could do absolutely nothing without the consent of his Wise Men [the Witan]. First of all, it was from them that he derived his political being, and it was on them that he depended for its continuance. The Witan chose the king and the Witan could depose him. The power of deposition is a power which, from its very nature, can be exercised but rarely; we therefore do not find many kings deposed by Act of Parliament either before or since the Norman Conquest. . . .

" If the Witan could depose the king, still more undoubtedly did the Witan elect the king. It is strange how people's eyes are blinded on this subject. . . . The ancient English Kingship was elective. It was elective in the same sense in which all the old Teutonic kingdoms were elective. Among a people in whose eyes birth was highly valued, it was deemed desirable that the king should be the descendant of illustrious and royal ancestors. In the days of heathendom it was held that the king should come of the supposed stock of the Gods. These feelings everywhere pointed to some particular house as the royal house, the house whose members had a special claim on the suffrages of the electors. In every kingdom there was a royal family, out of which alone, under all ordinary circumstances, kings were chosen; but within that royal family the Witan of the land had a free choice."

Freeman had it in mind to refute the old Tory doctrine of the Divine Right of kings. He points out that there have been an infinite number of different rules of succession in different countries; that it is absurd to suppose that any one of these is more natural or eternal than another. What is strange is that he should assume that the English law was always clear and coherent, even if it changes at certain times. He lived, as do we, under a monarchy whose rules of succession were precisely defined by law: they are, perhaps, the most precise and clear-cut arrangements surrounding our modern sovereigns. When a king or queen dies, we know who is going to succeed—or rather, who has instantly succeeded; the whole royal family is arranged in order of succession, according to a coherent principle established by law; in this case by written, Statute Law.

In the early Middle Ages the law of England was unwritten. There are exceptions to this statement, as we shall see; but they do not affect our present problem. This means that succession to the throne was arranged by custom and tradition. Custom can be a very definite thing, and very tenacious; but among primitive peoples it has a way of appearing definite and clear only to the people who operate, live and assume it; of appearing to the outsider vague, indefinite, even contradictory. A special difficulty attaches to the study of early monarchies: as time passed, practices changed, but our information is often so slender that we must try to draw a clue from here and there and form a coherent picture covering a wide space of time. A further difficulty is that at various times there was much diversity of opinion, more than has commonly been allowed; and since the succession to the throne was always a vital issue, it was frequently the subject of discussion and debate.

There were, indeed, no precise rules; but the succession to the thrones of the Anglo-Saxon kingdoms and the English kingdom was hedged round with a series of conventions, customs and assumptions; and out of the dialectic between these conventions each succession was settled—sometimes peacefully, sometimes by violence. Frequently a "strong man armed" seized the throne; and in later centuries at least he often felt bound to justify his action, and from the way in which he justified it we can tell what rules he was pretending to have followed. If at all possible, he showed that he was related to his predecessor—that he had a hereditary claim; he argued that the people had accepted his rule in due form—that he had been "elected", whatever that meant; and he asserted that his predecessor had declared that he was to succeed—he had been designated by a reigning king. Our investigation of king-making must be woven out of these three threads, inheritance, election and designation; in some way or another each of these three entered into most acts of king-making in western Europe in the Middle Ages.

Freeman spoke as if a king was elected, as if monarchy was essentially elective; inheritance was respected, election was the law. This is a large and strange assumption; and we must be very wary of making assumptions.

Even the most obvious generalisation about kingship, that only one person rules at a time, had numerous exceptions to it. In early days kings did not necessarily rule alone: they may indeed not normally have done so. All the male members of a family could rule together, while one king might hold a pre-eminence, so it appears, in most kingdoms. As time passed "monarchy" in the literal sense—the rule of one man —steadily developed. In later times the Anglo-Saxon monarchies remained hereditary; not in the sense that the kingdom passed by any strict rule of primogeniture, from eldest son to eldest son, but that in the large majority of cases a king was in fact succeeded by his eldest son or nearest male relative. There are cases in which a brother succeeded although the old king had children; but usually in such cases the children were very young. There are one or two cases when it was argued that a son "born in the purple"—when his father was king—had a superior right to one born before his father succeeded; and none of the Norman kings was the heir by "primogeniture". In 1066 Edgar the Ætheling was related to Edward the Confessor more nearly than William of Normandy, far more nearly than Harold. In 1087 and 1100 the Conqueror's younger sons, William and Henry, succeeded although their eldest brother Robert was alive. In 1135 Henry I's nephew Stephen succeeded, although Henry left a legitimate daughter, and Stephen himself had an elder brother.

The succession in 1066 and the succession in 1135 are among the most extraordinary and interesting in English history. They come near the end of our period, and so are relatively well documented; and they reveal between them almost all the problems and forces at work in English king-making. They will serve us very well as examples of the various conventions and assumptions.

Edward the Confessor (1042-66) was childless. He had a nephew called Edward who lived in exile in Hungary; a cousin called William who was duke of Normandy; while the most powerful man in England after the king was Harold, earl of Wessex, who was his brother-in-law. In addition, his predecessor, Harthacnut, who was also king of Denmark, had made an arrangement with Magnus, king of Norway, that, if either should die without an heir, the other was to succeed to his kingdom. In virtue of this Magnus had invaded Denmark and laid claim to England in 1042-3; and his claim was inherited (oddly enough) by his uncle, Harold Hardrada.

Edward's closest relation was his nephew; but Edward the exile died in 1057, and his son, Edgar the Ætheling, was too young to be a serious candidate in 1066. To William, on hereditary grounds, two objections could be raised: that he was illegitimate, and that he was related to Edward in the female line, and not himself descended from Edward's predecessors. It is abundantly clear that, if heredity had been in this instance the vital test, William would never have become king of England. It is strange enough that he ever became duke of Normandy: when his father died he was a boy of seven and the duchy was in uproar; and in the Middle Ages illegitimacy was normally regarded as a barrier to succession. He was the exception which proved all the rules; for the precedent was never followed. Henry I acknowledged at least twenty illegitimate children, including a number of sons; but none of them succeeded him.

The question whether the kingdom could pass through the female line is more complicated. The short answer seems to be that it had very rarely happened in Anglo-Saxon times, but that there was no known barrier against it. Women were on the whole more respectfully treated before the Conquest than after; but we must distinguish carefully between rules of succession and the status of women. Many societies have been "matrilineal", that is, inheritance has passed normally through a female line, but this does not necessarily, nor even usually, go with a high status for the womenfolk themselves. Nor can we deduce from the attitude to women in pre-Conquest times anything about the rules of inheritance. All that we can safely say is that it was possible for property to pass in the female line under Anglo-Saxon law, but not normal. All the Germanic peoples were mainly patrilineal; but in none of them, in early days, was this a strict rule. At one time anthropologists taught us that inheritance must be either patrilineal or matrilineal; and that, if we found traces of succession in the female line in a patrilineal society, it must mean that it had once been matrilineal. This view eventually seeped through to the historians, and one sometimes hears echoes of it still. But it has long been abandoned by the anthropologists: it is quite common for systems of inheritance to contain both elements.

It is possible that succession in the female line was less rare than our records suggest. It has been the practice in many societies for men, especially great men, to recite with pride the catalogue of their ancestors; genealogy has been a favourite form of literature (if such it can be called) in many parts of the world at many different times. The royal genealogies of primitive peoples are rarely historical documents, though they often enshrine—and may preserve for centuries—some elements of genuine tradition. Their purpose is to join the reigning king to the ancestor from whom the kingdom derives; in some cases, from the god who gave the kings their authority. It is in the nature of genealogies to suggest a tidy line of succession from father to son—to cover up more distant relationships, where necessary, and to jump generations. Since our early records of royal Saxon families are mainly genealogical, we may be inclined to exaggerate the patrilineal element in royal succession. But the influence of genealogies works both ways: from early days the love of genealogy inclined men to stick to the male line, to insist that a king should be the direct descendant of the ancestor who gave his name to the dynasty. In the early records of Wessex, it is frequently emphasised that this or that king was of the line of Cerdic; and almost all the Anglo-Saxon genealogies go back ostensibly to Woden, the chief God of the pagan Teutonic hierarchy.

It may have helped to give colour to William's claim to the throne that his great-aunt was Edward's mother. But it did not make William a descendant of Cerdic, still less of Woden. William's wife was of Cerdic's line; and his youngest son, Henry I, whose claim to be William's heir was doubtful, married Edgar the Ætheling's niece, Edith or Matilda, and once more brought the blood of Cerdic (and perhaps of Woden!) into the English royal house.

In fact, of course, William was king because he had succeeded in conquering the country; it was his strength, not his
right, which convinced the Witan that they must accept him.
Conquest and usurpation were comparatively common events
in the early Middle Ages; and the ease with which a disputed
succession could lead to civil war and bloodshed helps to
explain why archbishops and bishops were prepared to accept
and crown *de facto* kings, sometimes at very short notice:
they were trying to stifle dispute by presenting a *fait
accompli*. Already in the early eleventh century Swein of
Denmark and his son Cnut had been accepted and elected
kings simply because they had succeeded in conquering the
country. Election gave a cloak of legitimacy to a usurper,
and Cnut strengthened his position by marrying his predecessor's widow, which gave him affinity, though not kindred,
with the house of Cerdic. William the Conqueror went
further: he asserted, and believed, that he was king by right
as well as by conquest. Earl Harold had been Edward the
Confessor's brother-in-law, since Edward's queen was his
sister. But this hardly made him the king's next of kin; and
since Harold was elected, and succeeded against both Harold
Hardrada and (for a few months) against William of Normandy, it might be supposed that Freeman was right, and
that the monarchy was essentially elective. This, however,
would be a very superficial view of the case. Edward the
Confessor died on 5 January;[2] Harold was "elected" and
crowned on 6 January. It is quite impossible that the election
was anything but a formality: it must have been planned
before the old king's death. It is commonly supposed that a
monarchy is either hereditary or elective. This dilemma and
the facts of 1066 sit ill together. None of the three candidates had a hereditary claim which would stand any serious
inspection; the obvious "heir", Edgar the Ætheling, was
ignored until after the battle of Hastings. There was certainly a hereditary and an elective element in the English
monarchy; but these were factors in a more complex situation;
and to understand this, and the meaning of "election", we

[2] Or possibly on 4 January.

must make contact with a third factor, the most decisive of all.

After Hastings, William might claim to be king by divine judgement as well as by conquest. Neither aspect of his title was neglected. But even in the eleventh century men hesitated to assume, without further inquiry, on whose side God really wished to be; and even in the eleventh century men could distinguish between might and right. By what right was William king?

In all probability the claim which mattered most to the two Harolds and to William was essentially the same: that at various times and in various ways each had been designated heir to the kingdom by a reigning king. Harold Hardrada's designation was remote. His nephew and predecessor, Magnus, had made, as we have seen, an arrangement with Edward's predecessor by which if either died without an heir, the other should succeed to both kingdoms. We do not know precisely what these words meant: how close a relation was implied in the word " heir ", whether the kingdom of Harthacnut was meant to include England as well as Denmark, whether there was any intention that the arrangement should carry on to Magnus's successor. The claim may have been exceedingly shadowy; but there is no doubt of its nature. Harold Hardrada could only claim the English throne by virtue of designation by Harthacnut. In this the Witan, or Witenagemot, can have no place at all.

Duke William's claim was more lucid. He had been designated by Edward the Confessor as his heir. The Norman sources, not unnaturally, are more explicit on this than the English, and the story has been doubted. But it seems to be assumed in the Bayeux Tapestry. This shows us how Harold fell accidentally into William's hands in 1064, and how William made him swear a solemn oath. It does not define the oath, but clearly implies that Harold swore to support William's claim to the English throne. It is likely that William used strong pressure; but it seems to me unlikely that Harold would have sworn unless he was compelled to admit that William had a case; and equally improbable that William would have thought of invading England in 1066 unless he had a well-based claim to the throne. There seems only one explanation, that William had been designated formally by Edward as his heir. This is most likely to have happened when Edward was most his own master, and most able to indulge his taste of giving patronage to Normans— that is to say, in the years 1051-2. In 1051 an English source records a state visit to Edward by William, to a king by a foreign duke—a very rare and singular event in this period; we can hardly doubt that it was then that Edward promised him the crown. (See p. 203)

How, then, did Harold succeed in 1066? Edward had designated William as his heir. The Witan, or the leading factions in it, may never have been happy about William's claim; they may well have been openly opposed to it in 1065-6. Harold had by then established himself as the leading man in the country, the person most likely to hold England together and defend it successfully against Norwegian attack. But we have seen that Harold's "election" was purely formal. The decision must have been taken in Edward's lifetime. The English sources state quite plainly that Edward granted the kingdom to Harold, and some such story is also implied by one Norman chronicler—who goes on to point out that this was either untrue or unjust, since Edward had already granted it to William. In the Bayeux Tapestry (*figure 9f*) King Edward's burial has been placed before his death, so as to enable the scene headed "Here King Edward addresses his faithful followers in his bed" to be placed side by side with one headed "Here they gave the king's crown to Harold". The inscription, as so often, is elliptical; the interpretation, in the circumstances of the eleventh century, is clear. Edward had designated Harold as his successor.

This implication could be drawn even if it were not supported by other evidence. There is copious evidence, from all over Western Europe, that designation by the old king was a crucial element in the making of the new. Conrad I of Germany designated Henry of Saxony, founder of the great Saxon dynasty, as his successor (919), although they were in no way related. In German history before 1077 this was the normal process, although a man could not reign until he had been acknowledged as king by representatives of his subjects. Charlemagne had designated and crowned his son Louis the Pious in his own lifetime, so that there were two kings and two emperors in Charles's last years. This plan of establishing a successor in one's own lifetime, had already been tried by Offa, the king of Mercia, in the late eighth century; and was often to be followed in England, France and Spain. In the early eighth century Bede tells us that one English king handed over his kingdom to his successor, another decided who was to succeed him. These cases are few, but the cases in which we have any details about how kings succeeded are also few.

Freeman's account of the Witan is now seen to be profoundly misleading. Its rights are much more doubtful, and were probably more vague by far than he allowed. The Witan consisted of those leading men and counsellors (so far as we can tell) whom the king chose to summon; it advised him, but only when he asked its advice. On the other hand a king was wise to ask and take advice; and a king who was on good terms with his Witan would find it easier to enforce his will, and be much more in touch with the temper of his subjects. It may well be that "designation" played a larger part in king-making than election; but we must not abolish the Witan altogether. If we ask "Why did King Edward change his mind?" we are faced with a very awkward question; so awkward that some historians have averred that he cannot have changed his mind, and that some part of the story must be untrue. This seems to be unnecessary scepticism, although I do not think we can be sure what happened in the Christmas court of 1065. The king was old and ill; he may have been more open to influence than hitherto. He may have felt that Harold was the one man strong enough to save the kingdom from chaos, and in particular to defend it against Harold Hardrada, the most noted warrior of the northern world. We may be fairly sure that he was under strong pressure from many of his subjects to prefer Harold to William. It is no doubt true that the " election " on 6 January was a formality; but only because the Wise Men had already made up their minds.

The " election " indeed seems usually to have been a purely formal process, however much lobbying may have lain behind it. It was hardly an election in our sense of the word. We assume in an election that there shall be more than one candidate; that there shall be a fixed and easily defined body of electors; and that the election shall be by some kind of majority vote. Between 450 and 1154, so far as we know, no election of this kind took place in Europe. The first known election under a majority principle took place in 1181, when Pope Lucius III was elected under the papal election decree passed at the Lateran council of 1179, which laid down (for the first time) that a majority of two-thirds among the cardinals made a man pope. In the " election " of kings there was no majority principle, no fixed body of electors, and very often only one candidate. Why, then, do we call them " elections " at all?

The word " elect " or " choose " (Latin *eligere*, Old English *ceosan*) was used by contemporaries so often as to make it plain that it played an important part in their thinking. There are, however, few more obscure words in English constitutional history. Clearly there was some difference of opinion among contemporaries. The well-known writer of the turn of the tenth and eleventh centuries, Abbot Ælfric, evidently felt that there was a real element of choice when a new king came to be made: " No man can make himself king, but the people has the choice to choose as king whom they please; but after he is consecrated as king, he then has dominion over the people, and they cannot shake his yoke from their necks." It is doubtful if either part of this statement would have been generally accepted at the time; the people did not " choose whom they please ", and every Germanic people claimed in some way or another the right to resist a tyrannical king, the right to rebel. We should not read too much into Ælfric's words: he is not stating precise constitutional doctrines, but telling his audience that kings ought not to be usurpers and people ought not to rebel—a general plea for good behaviour, not unsuitable in the reign of Ethelred the Unready.

The word " elect " was used in contexts where no element of choice can have been involved. Sometimes it was God who elected; and all kings felt themselves to be kings by God's grace—and so by his choice, by *His* election. But the word is also commonly used of human agents. When Henry I became king of Germany he was first designated by King Conrad on his deathbed, then, at the instance of Conrad's brother, " elected " by the Franks and Saxons. The Franks and Saxons were two of the four peoples who comprised his kingdom. They did not choose Henry as king, they simply acknowledged him; and there is little doubt that this is the true meaning of the Latin *eligere* and the Old English *ceosan* in English sources. In many cases these words may hide discussion and arrangement; what they actually describe is a formal process of acknowledgement and acclamation.

This comes out very clearly in the description of how Edmund Ironside became king in 1016. Cnut was master of a great part of England; Ethelred was dead. To rally support to Edmund, Ethelred's eldest son, demanded as impressive a show of king-making as could be staged. He was " chosen ", we are told, by the members of the Witan who were in London at the time, and the citizens (*burhwaru*) of London. From this and later occasions when the citizens of London played a part in king-making they came to make the startling claim that no king could be chosen without their consent. London was already a great city by 1016, and the leading men may have played an important part in the events of that year. But what was needed was a group to strengthen the Witan, only a proportion of whom can have been present, and a throng of citizens to acclaim the new king. The Witan and the leading citizens simply acknowledged their allegiance to Edmund; the people acclaimed him; that seems to have been all that was normally involved in an early medieval " election ".

In later times, and perhaps already, the coronation rite

opened with a formal demand for the people's consent. The archbishop presented, and still presents, the sovereign-elect to the people for their approval; and only when this had been signified did he proceed. This is not included in the earliest rite we possess, that for Edgar's coronation in 973; he had been a reigning king for fourteen years or so, and it was taken for granted that the people accepted him as king. We do not know when the presentation, the *collaudatio*, first entered the service, but it was clearly an established part of it by 1066. This is surely what Stigand is performing in the Bayeux Tapestry (*figure 10a*) on 6 January 1066; and this may have been all that was involved in Harold's election. More probably some formal gathering of notables, to whom one of the leading men, perhaps one of the archbishops, presented Harold, will have preceded it. Sometimes the two processes were kept well apart. After Hastings the Wise Men (by great folly, as one of the chroniclers thought) acknowledged Edgar the Ætheling; later Archbishop " Ealdred (of York), prince Edgar, Earl Edwin, Earl Morcar, and all the best men from London " went to Berkhamsted to submit to William and swear fealty; thus completing his " election ". Later, on Christmas Day, he was anointed and crowned in Westminster Abbey; and the great shout of the *collaudatio* at the opening of the service so frightened the Norman knights that they set fire to the buildings round the abbey church. But the seal was put on Edward's designation, William's conquest, the Witan's submission and God's election by the sacred ceremony of anointing and coronation, according to a rite which has much in common with that employed in 1953. Thus the *collaudatio* was originally the formal act of election; but in due course became a fossilised confirmation of a formal act which had already taken place.

The final act of the king-making was the solemn confirmation by God's blessing of the process which had gone before in the rites of anointing and coronation. All that we have described so far—inheritance, designation, and election—has a long history going back into early Germanic society. Some attempt shall be made a little later to penetrate into this obscure region. The history of the coronation ceremony, however, is comparatively clear. In the fifth and sixth centuries the ceremonies of election of Germanic kings were often completed by raising the king on a shield. We do not know whether this was ever done in England. Indeed, we have no idea what ceremonies were performed when a king was made before the days of Offa, little enough before the days of Edgar. In 787 Ecgfrith, Offa's son, was "consecrated" in his father's lifetime. This has been taken to mean anointed with chrism and holy oil, the central act of any medieval coronation ceremony. It is no coincidence that this should have happened in the late eighth century. In 751 the Frankish dynasty was changed by a ceremony of anointing and coronation sanctioned by the pope; in 781 two sons of Charlemagne had been anointed by the pope in person. What is the significance of these events?

The early Frankish kings had all been drawn from the family of the "Merovings". Whatever their origin, they had reigned so long by the eighth century that it was a considerable effort for anyone in Francia to imagine a king not of the dynasty—even though among the other European peoples Visigothic kings had usually been "elected" and Lombard kings had only had any sort of hereditary succession for about a century. In the early eighth century the effective ruler of Francia was the "mayor of the palace" Charles Martel; for a time he dispensed with monarchy altogether, but most of the time he kept a Merovingian puppet in being. In 751 his son Pippin grew weary of the Merovingian farce, and applied to the pope for permission to assume the royal title himself.

In such a situation it was natural for men in the Middle Ages, and especially churchmen of the eighth century, to look back into the Old Testament for precedents for what they were doing. And there they found what they were looking for: how Samuel had anointed David to be king because Saul had lost God's favour—even though David was in no way related to Saul; and how David's successor Solomon was chosen, not by primogeniture, but by "Zadok the priest and Nathan the prophet" (albeit acting on King David's instructions). The ceremony devised for Pippin's king-making was what we should call a coronation; like many Teutonic kings, he had taken over crown (or diadem), orb and sceptre from the ceremonial of the eastern Roman Empire. But the crucial event in it was the anointing. This was performed, in medieval coronations, with holy oil and with chrism; and chrism (oil and balsam mixed) was also used in the ordination of priests and the consecration of bishops. Small wonder that anointing came to be regarded as having a sacramental character, as a kind of ordination.

Some kind of anointing may have been known among the Celtic princes of Ireland and Wales before the days of Offa. But we know little of this, and little enough of the ceremonies of king-making between Offa's time and Edgar's. In 973, at the age of 30—the canonical age at which a man might be consecrated bishop—and at the height of his power, Edgar was solemnly anointed and crowned. We have records of the ceremony performed by St. Dunstan of Canterbury and St. Oswald of York at Bath on Whit Sunday 973. The same order was used down to the mid- or late-eleventh century; and many elements in it were used in 1953.

"The holy season [of Pentecost] was approaching", writes a contemporary, "in which it was the custom for the archbishops and all the other eminent bishops and abbots, and religious abbesses, and ealdormen and reeves and other laymen" to come to court. "An edict went out from the emperor that they should come to him, from the east, from the west, from the north, and from the sea." They came not to expel him or to plot against him, "as the wretched Jews had once treated the kind Jesus"; but rather "that the most reverent bishops might bless, anoint, consecrate him, by Christ's leave, from whom and by whom the blessed unction of highest blessing and holy religion has proceeded"—the first of many indications of what is implicit in the words of the service itself, that the king is God's elect, God's chosen, and for this reason only (whatever the human instruments) fit to be God's anointed.

Two bishops led Edgar into the church while the choir sang

an antiphon. The king prostrated himself before the altar, laid aside the crown (which he already wore), and Dunstan began the singing of the *Te Deum*, but was so moved by the occasion that he wept for joy at the king's humility and wisdom. When the *Te Deum* was finished, the bishops raised the king, and the archbishop administered to him the coronation oath. At this time, the king swore: " that the Church of God and all his Christian people shall keep true peace under our rule at all times; that I shall forbid thefts and every iniquity to every grade of man; that I shall ordain justice and mercy in all judgements, that the kindly and merciful God may grant to me and to you his mercy "—and to this all present said " Amen ". After three prayers, came the solemn prayer calling down God's blessing " on your servant Edgar, whom we have chosen with suppliant devotion for royal authority over Angles and Saxons ", and asking God to grant him the faithfulness of Abraham, the gentleness of Moses, the fortitude of Joshua, the humility of David, the wisdom of Solomon, and to help to nourish, instruct, fortify and build up the church of his kingdom and all the people committed to him, ending with the anointing by Dunstan in Christ's name, and the antiphon " Zadok the priest and Nathan the prophet " which is still in use, though now in English, not in Latin.

In the midst of further prayers, the king was given a ring and sword, symbols of royal power; then he was crowned, and sceptre and staff were placed in his hands; and a blessing pronounced over him. Then the king received the allegiance of his leading subjects, and was acclaimed: " *vivat rex, vivat rex, vivat rex in eternum* "; and his royal position defined: " Stand and grasp your royal status, which you have held till now at your father's designation (*paterna suggestione*),[8] delegated to you by hereditary right on the authority of almighty God and by the present agency of ourselves, God's bishops and other servants; and the nearer you see the clergy standing to the holy altars, the stronger the honour you should remember to give them . . ., so that the mediator of God and

[8] Edgar succeeded his brother, not his father, and this phrase should not be interpreted too literally.

men may confirm you on the throne of this kingdom as mediator of clergy and people, and make you reign with him in the eternal kingdom—Jesus Christ, to wit, Our Lord. . . ." And after further prayers, and the anointing or " consecration " of the queen, the ceremonies were completed by a solemn mass.

From the time of Edgar it was normal for the queen to be crowned with her husband; and the *Life* of Edward the Confessor, in describing how Queen Edith used to sit at his feet, notes that a throne was always set for her beside the king, according to custom, even though she rarely occupied it. It seems, however, that queens had not always been so respectfully treated. Asser (late ninth century) describes how the West Saxons in his day refused to allow the queen to sit beside the king, or to take the title queen (*regina*); she was only the king's wife. This he attributes to the misbehaviour of a daughter of Offa king of Mercia who was for a time queen of Wessex. Whether the story is true is quite uncertain; but it is likely enough that Offa's daughter was remembered as the symbol of the subjection of Wessex to Mercia in Offa's time (late eighth century), and that queens were subjected to a temporary and local disfavour as a result. In general, however, women were treated with high respect in pre-Conquest England, and it is from Wessex at an earlier date that we have our one example of an Anglo-Saxon queen taking over the reins of government. In 672, the *Anglo-Saxon Chronicle* tells us " Cenwalh [king of Wessex] passed away, and Seaxburh, his queen, reigned one year after him." Her rule did not last long (we do not know what brought it to an end), and queens were normally regarded as consorts simply; but when the rites of coronation developed, they were reckoned to share their husbands' regality in some measure at least, and so Edgar's queen was anointed and crowned.

By a ceremony in all essentials the same, with the *collaudatio* added, muted by the confusion without, and lacking the queen's consecration, since William's wife was still safe in Normandy, the dramatic problem of who should succeed Edward the Confessor was finally resolved on Christmas Day 1066. To understand it we have had to consider the attitude of Edward, of his subjects, of William's rivals—and finally of God himself, as understood by the English bishops. William won his kingdom by force of arms; but he claimed to be king by right, and in order to do so, he had to make his claim as clear as it could be. He was related to Edward, but not very closely, and to earlier members of his line not at all. His hereditary claim was better than Harold's, but not strikingly good. He was elected, but only in a purely formal sense; the English leaders submitted to the conqueror. The strength of his case lay in the attitude of Edward the Confessor: Edward had declared William his successor (even if he had changed his mind since), and Harold had sworn to accept William. In 1066, the principle of designation was more powerful than inheritance or "election". In our second example, the accession of King Stephen, the elements are in rather different proportions; but the events of his accession illustrate very clearly the operations of the three principles of inheritance, election and designation, and so form a fitting close to our investigation of king-making.

On 1 December 1135 King Henry was "alive and dead", in Lyons-la-Forêt in Normandy. Following the precedent set by William II, Henry's nephew Stephen of Blois, count of Boulogne, crossed the Channel, convinced the archbishop of Canterbury that he was the true heir and had Henry's dying vote, and was crowned king, probably on 22 December. In 1139 Henry's daughter Matilda, widow of the Emperor Henry V and now countess of Anjou—whose supporters were therefore called "Angevins"—also crossed the Channel, and adherents gathered round her. For a moment, in 1141, she was mistress of London, and victory seemed in her grasp. But she failed, and passed on her claim to her son; the young Henry invaded England in 1147, again in 1149, again in 1153, was finally accepted by Stephen as his heir in 1153, and himself crowned on 19 December 1154.

The events of the "anarchy" raised much comment, and we have a variety of statements from supporters of both sides: chroniclers, like Stephen's supporter who wrote the *Gesta Stephani*, or Matilda's supporter, William of Malmesbury, gave the practical arguments produced in 1135 with the echo of later comments wrapped up in their own reflections. In 1139 the issue was debated before the pope, and of this we have two reports, from John of Salisbury in his *Memoirs of the Papal Court*, and from an eye witness, Gilbert Foliot, later abbot of Gloucester and ultimately bishop of London (1163-87). Gilbert, an ardent supporter of the empress, adds the teeming arguments of a fertile legal brain, which soar to the heights of law natural and divine.

In the early stages only two candidates were seriously considered; but it is interesting to reflect that these emerged from a possible bag of at least six. Matilda was Henry I's only surviving legitimate child. If a woman could succeed, her hereditary claim was clearly very strong. Stephen's advocate before the pope claimed, indeed, that she was illegitimate; that her mother had taken a nun's vows at Romsey Abbey and was therefore not free to marry her father, and so she must be set aside. As Matilda's supporters reasonably pointed out, the saintly Archbishop Anselm had himself looked into this and allowed them to marry, and the pope had confirmed his decision. Nor had anyone dared to raise this hint in Henry's lifetime; twice, indeed, the English baronage had sworn allegiance to Matilda as their future queen. On the first occasion Stephen, the legitimate nephew, and Robert of Gloucester, the illegitimate son, had competed as to which of them should be the first lay baron after the king of Scots to swear the oath. These oaths were reluctant, and the first, in many folk's eyes, was rendered null by the subsequent marriage (without baronial consent) of Matilda to the count of Anjou. There was precedent for royal widows helping to decide the succession, as in Beowulf and in the Danish legend well known to us from Shakespeare's *Hamlet*, and, more strikingly, in the case of Queen Emma, wife successively to Ethelred II and Cnut. This might encourage the idea that a royal daughter, who carried royal blood in her veins, might settle a succession. But it was assumed that Matilda's husband would rule, not she herself. A recent precedent for a woman ruling in her own right could be found in Queen Urraca, successor to Alphonso VI of León-Castile; but it was an exceptional case and had not been a success. It was generally expected that the crown would pass through Matilda's husband to her sons. Succession in the female line had its peculiar rules; but these raised no special difficulty in the present case, since all the other claimants bar one owed their claim to a lady.

The one exception was Robert of Gloucester, who seems to have been considered. He refused, however, to be a candidate, on the ground that he was illegitimate, and this barrier seems to have been generally accepted, in spite of the obvious precedent of William the Conqueror. Earl Robert is recorded to have preferred the claims of his nephew Henry, son of Matilda and Count Geoffrey. Henry was two years old in 1135, and, even if his claims had been seriously considered, adult direction was needed to deal with the crisis which developed. It is doubtful if the idea of inheritance, powerful though it was, had yet progressed so far as to outweigh "suitability" in most people's minds. Minors had succeeded in the tenth century; the Conqueror as duke of Normandy had been a minor; but England was not to have a boy-king again until 1216.

If Matilda's claims were to be accepted, the obvious candidate was Geoffrey, count of Anjou, her husband; a worthy heir of the savage counts of Anjou, the man most likely to show the strength of Henry I. There were, however, certain difficulties. First of all, Anjou and Normandy were traditional enemies; the idea of being subject to a count of Anjou was not in the least congenial to the Anglo-Norman baronage. In the second place, he would rule as Matilda's husband; but the marriage was so unhappy that it was extremely doubtful whether they would be able to live together peacefully enough to rule their great dominions. By a curious chance, however, they had sufficiently patched up their differences in Henry I's last years to spend a short space together, to have children, and to quarrel with Henry. The count of Anjou was suspect in England; in 1135 he and his wife were at war against Henry.

Henry's other near relative was his sister, the countess of
Blois, who was still alive: she died in 1137. No one seems to
have considered the countess herself, but her two eldest sons,
Theobald and Stephen, were among the strongest candidates.
Theobald was count of Blois, Champagne and Chartres; one
of the greatest lords of northern France. He would at least
have the strength to hold the power of Anjou at bay, and the
Norman barons proceeded to invite him to be their duke.
While they were preparing to acknowledge their allegiance to
him, however, they received a message that Theobald's
younger brother, Stephen, count of Boulogne, and (owing to
King Henry's favour) probably the best endowed English
baron, was crossing the Channel. Theobald was a trifle
querulous, but refused to queer his brother's pitch. And so
Stephen was able, like William II, to win the archbishop of
Canterbury and have himself crowned, like Henry I, to seize
the treasury at Winchester, like Edmund—and this is strongly
emphasised by his biographer—to win the voice of the citizens
of London, who made great capital out of an occasion on
which, as in 1016, the loud voice of the London citizens was
needed to hide the small numbers of the nobles who
" elected " the king. His wife, like Henry I's, was of the old
English line: a niece of Henry's queen and Edgar the Ætheling,
daughter of a Scottish princess.

We have seen that Henry I, in earlier years, had publicly
and strenuously designated Matilda his heiress. After his
death the story was told that like Edward the Confessor he
had changed his mind, and on his deathbed designated
Stephen. This story has generally been disbelieved; but it was
one of the two crucial issues in 1135 and the years immediately
following, and the central mystery of Stephen's accession.

The other great issue was that of suitability: Matilda was
difficult and quarrelsome, too inclined to remember that she
had been an empress; her husband was distrusted by the
Normans. Stephen, on the other hand, was a leader among
the barons, one of themselves, open-hearted, brave, energetic,
innocent of his uncle's rapacity and perhaps of his uncle's

cruelty. This alone might account in fair measure for his success; at least it may explain why he won support. But it fails to explain the most puzzling feature of the events of 1135: the rapid and decisive action which he took after Henry's death. He was crowned as quickly as Rufus had been, and against much heavier odds. Stephen was always capable of rapid action; but in later years lacked the determination and persistence to carry his actions to success. It is possible, as most historians have thought, that for once in his life Stephen saw his chance, and took it; that his rapidity of action was sufficient both to carry him to temporary success, and to push his elder brother into the background without even the trouble of an argument. It is possible; but there is another explanation.

John of Salisbury tells us that in the argument before the pope in 1139, the king's advocate, Arnulf, later bishop of Lisieux, alleged two arguments: that Matilda was illegitimate, and that Henry on his deathbed had changed his mind and designated Stephen. " And he declared that this had been proved publicly before the English church to William, archbishop of Canterbury and legate of the holy see, by the oath of Earl Hugh [Bigod] and two knights; and that on hearing the proof the archbishop had recognised Stephen's claim to the crown with the unanimous consent and approval of the bishops and nobles. What had been done with such ceremony, could not, he concluded, be undone." In answer the empress's advocate countered the charge of illegitimacy, and denied that Henry had changed his mind: " As for your statement that the king changed his mind, it is proved false by those who were present at the king's death. Neither you nor Hugh could possibly know his last requests, since neither was there." Nor could the archbishop's acceptance hurt the empress, since she—to whom they had all sworn so solemnly —was condemned to the loss of her crown without being given any chance to answer the charges against her case. Gilbert Foliot is only explicit about the argument on the empress's legitimacy. This is what especially concerned him, since his case is based almost entirely on the hereditary claim of the empress. But he does discuss the question whether a father can disinherit a legitimate heir, to which his answer is: only for rebellion or the like, and he firmly (though erroneously) asserts that the empress was never guilty of this.[4] The argument may be academic; but it is likely that implicit in it was the charge of the royal advocate that Henry had abandoned his daughter on his deathbed. In any case we may probably take John of Salisbury's word for it that this argument was in men's minds. John was writing under Henry II, the empress's son: he had no motive for improving Stephen's case—save perhaps to discredit Stephen's advocate, a special enemy of John's. Whether the story was true is another matter. The earliest of the chroniclers, Orderic Vitalis (1141), William of Malmesbury and John of Worcester (c. 1142) make no mention of the story that Henry changed his mind on his deathbed. But William and John owed allegiance to the empress when they wrote.

Stephen's biographer, writing, it seems, early in Henry II's reign, arrives at a curious compromise. The enterprise was of Stephen's own devising; on arrival in England he was immediately elected by the citizens of London—and we are treated to a lecture on London's rights, in which the author, to put it mildly, doth protest too much. We are then told at length of a debate before the archbishop of Canterbury, whose decision, as first counsellor and as the man who would anoint the new king, was vital. The archbishop objected that he had sworn allegiance to Matilda. The answer to this is very strange indeed. Henry's design in extracting the oath and marrying his daughter to Anjou was to make peace between Anjou and Normandy. This laudable project, which makes Henry I out as a disinterested Nobel prizewinner, raised a difficulty: he knew the barons swore unwillingly. And so on his deathbed, to prevent his little scheme troubling them for ever, he released them from their oath. It is a mistake to take too

4 One would like to know how Gilbert Foliot described the empress's activities in 1135. Perhaps he drew a distinction between conniving at her husband's offensive activities and actual rebellion; perhaps he had conveniently forgotten the affair.

seriously speeches in medieval chronicles: direct speech was regularly used as a device to give colour and drama, to enable the actors or the author to comment; no one supposed them to be stenographically accurate. But they are often, none the less, extremely interesting; and this argument has a kind of logic of its own which has never, apparently, been observed. Henry's motive is patently absurd. If peace was his aim, he needed to tie his barons by every possible oath on his death-bed. But in fact the Angevin marriage was no guarantee of peace, with Anjou or within his own dominions, in his life-time. Nor has the ideal of peace for its own sake anything in common with Henry I as we know him; it is simply an emanation of the legendary Henry I, the " lover of peace " to whom men looked back, nostalgically, from the chaos of the succeeding reign. The story is ridiculous; and yet some story is urgently needed. The archbishop's arguments against Stephen are cogent; how then was he induced to crown him?

The *Gesta* tells us that Henry released his barons from their oath to Matilda on his deathbed, a story elaborated by later chroniclers. If this is all he did—if he released them without indicating who was to succeed, he acted either as a convinced democrat or in a fit of total irresponsibility. The former is impossible; the latter, for Henry I of all people, incredible. It is much more likely that the *Gesta* is repeating the old story that Henry designated Stephen on his deathbed, in a somewhat veiled form. But why is it veiled? When the *Gesta* was written, or at any rate finished, Henry II was on the throne.[5] In its later pages, Henry is always referred to as " the lawful heir ", even though Stephen's elder son lived to

[5] Since this was written, Prof. R. H. C. Davis has published a brilliant article on the authorship of the *Gesta Stephani* (*English Historical Review*, LXXVII (1962), 209-32), in which he argues that the earlier sections were completed in or about 1148, and not substantially revised later. The case for this is cogent; but it seems likely that some of the more vital sections, such as this, would have been retouched in the final revision, which must have taken place after Henry II's accession. Few things would have been more unwelcome to Henry II than to be told that Henry I had designated Stephen. Mr. Davis's argument, however, certainly raises a doubt about my explanation of the obscurity of the *Gesta*.

1153, his younger to 1159. This explains a curious element of prevarication in the book: it is in the main a panegyric of Stephen, but written by somebody who has had to come to terms with Angevin government. He cannot say openly that Henry I repudiated his daughter and her issue, for Henry II claimed above all to be his grandfather's heir. Yet if he says nothing about Henry I's deathbed, Stephen's case is gravely weakened.

Thus we have the Angevin chroniclers ranged on one side; Stephen's advocates on the other. The Angevins had a powerful motive for suppressing any story that Henry had designated Stephen; Stephen's supporters an equally strong motive for pressing it. Orderic, writing in a Normandy which had abandoned Stephen, gives no hint of it; perhaps his silence tells slightly against it. But in the main, we have here, as not uncommonly, a plain contradiction in the sources; and it is only by observing the behaviour of the main actors that we can hope to settle the issue.

Stephen acted with the utmost promptitude; the archbishop of Canterbury argued, but agreed. The king of France supported Stephen; the pope confirmed his coronation. The count of Blois withdrew his claims; the count and countess of Anjou did nothing; the earl of Gloucester, after a long pause, swore fealty to Stephen. Much of this reflects recognition of facts as they were. Disputed successions were common; acts of violent usurpation not rare. Normally the *fait accompli* had to be accepted, even by the Church, since the Church's refusal could only lead to bloodshed. What mattered to the pope was to keep England free from civil war. As for the king of France and the count of Blois, we know too little of the detailed circumstances to judge of their motives; but Theobald had little to hope for in England in any event, Louis everything to fear in France if Anjou was joined to Normandy.

The promptitude of Stephen and the acquiescence of Canterbury are the most remarkable points in this sequence of events. Stephen acted so fast that his manœuvre must almost certainly have been premeditated; it is indeed likely that it was inspired by a stronger personality than his own. The archbishop must have been convinced by cogent arguments. Both parts of the puzzle would be explained if Stephen could indeed bring testimony that Henry on his deathbed had designated him his heir.

There are, however, two other points to be taken into the account. The archbishop was concerned to provide England with an effective king who could prevent bloodshed: civil war was imminent; he might well feel that Stephen was more suitable, more capable of winning support than the empress. Stephen was a good soldier, and already well endowed in England. Nor was he slow to make promises of good rule and obedience to the Church. Stephen may well have seemed suitable, *idoneus*, a vital factor in the Church's eyes.

If Stephen's actions surprise us, and we look for a stronger personality to inspire him, his uncle is not our only choice. Another Henry, Stephen's younger brother, abbot of Glastonbury and bishop of Winchester, played a leading part in the events of Stephen's reign. He was not always on his brother's side, but William of Malmesbury attributes to him Stephen's early success: and makes his influence responsible for the archbishop's acquiescence. William's picture, in general, is confirmed by the *Gesta*. The brilliant, turbulent, ambitious Henry may well have influenced both his elder brothers; and we may accept William of Malmesbury's word that he hoped (and no doubt convinced the archbishop) that Stephen would prove a worthy guardian of the Church, and submit to the direction of his leading bishops.

Finally, is it credible that Henry I himself should have deserted his daughter after all his elaborate schemes, and declared for his nephew? It is clear that Henry had been seriously worried about the succession to his throne for many years: he had married again, but had no children by his second wife; he had summoned Matilda back from Germany against her will; he had exacted two oaths from his barons. In all this he seems to have been guided as much by a particular notion of inheritance as by affection. One would have expected his heart to have lain with his illegitimate son Earl

Robert or his legitimate nephew Stephen, both of whom he endowed with the best lands he had to give, to an almost unprecedented degree. He treated them with every mark of favour and affection, hunted with them, enjoyed their company. In contrast, he treated his daughter as a pawn in the marriage game, as so many women were treated in that age. At seven she was shipped to Germany; as a young widow she was hurried back, made heir to the throne, married forcibly to a younger man whom she despised (he was a mere count), and who had no liking for her. So her father allowed her to leave her husband; then reunited them so as to ensure that his line was continued with a supply of heirs. Finally, and not surprisingly, she spited the old man: rebellion broke out in Normandy, the count openly supported it, the empress only a little less openly fomented it.

What happened on Henry's deathbed is pure conjecture. If he felt that his daughter had shown herself " ungrateful "— had he not laden her with honours, made her an empress, promised her a kingdom?—that would be only understandable. He was an irascible member of an irascible line; he was capable of saying anything when the fit was on him. It is intelligible that he should succumb to a temporary reaction, a feeling that he might after all follow his heart not his head; that Stephen was Henry himself *redivivus*, a younger son married to a descendant of Alfred and Cerdic, and Woden.

When Queen Elizabeth I was on her deathbed, gargantuan efforts had to be made to get her to designate James as her successor. So precise was she about her prerogative, and so little did she relish thoughts of her own death, that she put the act off to the very last moment. In the end, an incoherent sign made after she was incapable of speech was interpreted as consent, and the last barrier to James's succession was removed. Around Henry's deathbed were gathered men passionately concerned about who should succeed. The leading men at Henry's deathbed named by Orderic were somewhat slow to join or support Stephen. Hugh Bigod claimed to have Henry's word that Stephen should succeed, but the empress's supporters rejoined that Hugh was not present at the deathbed. It is perfectly possible, however, that Hugh was near at hand, picked up a rumour that Stephen had been designated heir, and carried it at once to Boulogne, where (so it seems) Stephen then was; and with this rumour stirred Stephen to his remarkable adventure. It is likely, I think, that Stephen thought himself to have Henry's support. Whether Henry had wished to give it we shall never know.

In Germany in the late eleventh and twelfth centuries there were signs that inheritance and designation might one day give way to election as the means of creating a new king; and in the thirteenth and fourteenth centuries this came to pass: a specific body of electors made free choice—choice so free that in the early sixteenth century the kings of England, France and Spain could all be thought of as suitable candidates. In England and France this never happened. The word "election" was freely used; Stephen gave out that he had been elected by clergy and people, and the *Gesta* makes his election a key event. But he was "elected" by the citizens of London, not the Witan; and if Stephen could be thought of as an "elected" monarch, the precedent was not encouraging. In fact other ideas were more strongly present in people's minds: designation was still, perhaps, the most vital factor of all; inheritance was gaining ground, and being supplemented by sophisticated arguments from Roman and Canon Law; nor could any responsible person overlook the problem of whether the candidate was suitable for the office. Laymen and churchmen were agreed that the royal office was vital for the welfare of the people; the choice of a new king was a profoundly serious matter: too serious to be subjected to simple rules; so long as the English kings ruled as well as reigned, there was an element of uncertainty about the principles of succession. Strange as it may seem, the modern law of succession dates only from the eighteenth century.

CHAPTER III

THE OCCUPATIONS OF A KING

We have seen how kings were made; we have still to study how they lived: to provide them with palaces and retinues, to clothe and feed them, and fill their daily round.

The bulk of the surviving literature of Saxon and Norman times was written by churchmen, and written in Latin, the international language of the Church of western Christendom. Kings were usually illiterate. To this, as we shall see, there were notable exceptions; but it remains true that most laymen were not interested in book-learning, and that the surviving literature reflects the tastes and interests of the clergy. They have much to tell us of layfolk, but it comes to us at one remove; if we wish to make direct contact with laymen, we must look to the physical remains—houses, weapons, coins—unearthed by the spade, and the vernacular literature composed for them, for minstrels to recite in the great halls of kings and thegns in the evenings. This was essentially not a written but a spoken literature, passed down from minstrel to minstrel, alternately refined and corrupted in the crucible of human memory. The result is that only a small proportion ever came to be committed to parchment, and of what was written down only a part survives. The student of English history is relatively fortunate. Of French vernacular literature virtually nothing survives before the late eleventh century—though from then on it is abundant; of German literature only a little survives before 1100; a fair quantity of early Scandinavian poetry was written down in Iceland about the year 1250, and is known to us from later copies; but England can boast some 30,000 lines of Anglo-Saxon verse, quite apart from the substantial remains of Old English prose.

Much of this verse is religious: paraphrases of parts of the Bible, pious legends, saints' lives, spiritual fantasies like the famous *Dream of the Rood*. The men who wrote the manuscripts in which the poetry survives were themselves church-men, and the high proportion of religious verse in what they wrote no doubt in part reflects their tastes. But it is clear that it also reflects the tastes of many of the laymen for whom these poems were written. There is also some secular poetry; most notable of all the short epic *Beowulf*, the only complete survivor of the Germanic lays and epics of the early Middle Ages. *Beowulf* may well be uncharacteristic, in certain respects, of the literature from which it sprang—above all in being, as we shall see, a Christian poem with a Christian moral; but it reveals in vivid fashion much that we should not otherwise clearly perceive about the life of kings and the aspirations of their followers. Its date is not precisely known: it is normal to ascribe it to the eighth century, and it can hardly be later.

The poem opens with the death of a Danish king. " Scyld's hour came when he was in the prime of his strength. After a long reign the king departed into the care of God. His dearest retainers carried the beloved Danish leader to the sea's edge, as he had commanded while he could yet speak. Rime-crusted and ready to sail, a royal vessel with curved prow lay in harbour. They set down their dear king amidships, close by the mast. A mass of treasure was brought there from distant parts. No ship, they say, was ever so well equipped with swords, corselets, weapons, and armour. On the king's breast rested a heap of jewels which were to go with him far out into the keeping of the sea. The Danes furnished Scyld Scefing with offerings from their treasury that were as good as the gifts provided by those who, when he was a child, launched him alone across the ocean. High overhead they set his golden standard; then, surrendering him to the sea, they sadly allowed it to bear him off. And no one, whether a counsellor in hall or a soldier in the field, can truly say who received that cargo."

Until about twenty years ago this passage read to most readers like pure fantasy. But in 1939, shortly before the outbreak of the Second World War, the " harbour " into which just such a ship had sailed was excavated on a windy hill above the River Deben in Suffolk. It had long been known that the East Saxon kings had had one of their principal palaces at Rendlesham, four miles away; and excavation of the burial mounds, or barrows, at Sutton Hoo itself had begun in the previous year. One of the mounds had already revealed a ship burial, but this had been previously excavated by robbers, and its main contents are lost. In 1939 work began on one of the largest of the barrows, and once again the traces of a ship were found. Then the excavators began to look in its centre, where the burial chamber should be, hardly hoping to find it still intact. As they approached it, they realised that something of interest lay underneath—sufficient for them to halt their work, and call in a team of the most highly qualified experts to complete an extremely delicate task. Through the July days of 1939, as the war clouds gathered, gold and silver and jewellery, some of it of great beauty, the whole of unprecedented splendour and interest, were scooped from the centre of the ship. The owner of Sutton Hoo presented them to the nation; they were deposited in the British Museum, sorted and catalogued, and stowed safely away. Then the war came, and serious work was held up till it was over; for five years the experts and the not-so-expert speculated and guessed. Then the treasures were reopened and examined afresh, and proceeded to confound some of the speculation. They were examined and reconstructed in the laboratory, compared with other finds, analysed by archæologists, numismatists and historians. This process is still not complete, and the remaining mounds at Sutton Hoo still guard their secrets. (See p. 203)

The burial chamber contained armour, bowls, spoons and dishes, and various other objects. But it contains no body; and this has deepened the mystery of whom it was meant to celebrate.

It could be the tomb of a king. Scyld's boat was laden much like the boat at Sutton Hoo. True, it was not buried, but sent out to sea. But we know that burial was normal—a barrow was made for Beowulf himself at the end of the poem; and other ship burials have been found elsewhere, most notably in Sweden. We know too that the hero of Sutton Hoo was no ordinary mortal. Numerous Anglo-Saxon graves have been excavated; few of them have even the dignity of mounds raised above them; none of them so far compares with Sutton Hoo; nothing quite so splendid has yet been excavated anywhere in the Teutonic world. Mr. Boffin in *Our Mutual Friend* is described as the golden dustman, because of the great wealth he had inherited as heir to substantial piles of valuable dust. One might almost call Sutton Hoo the golden dustbin of the early medieval world, for its treasures are cosmopolitan. The lost warrior had spoons from the Byzantine Empire; bowls from Byzantium and Egypt; helmet, shield and sword from Sweden; the clasps and buckles of his harness, and the lid of his purse, were masterpieces of Anglo-Saxon jewellery; the money in his purse came from Merovingian Gaul (i.e. France). We cannot be sure that this represents his personal gear: when Beowulf himself was buried, an earlier treasure was looted to provide him with suitable equipment. But the money at least is a homogeneous collection, though not English, and reveals to the expert on coins that the burial took place about 650-60.

It is usually assumed that the lost warrior was in fact a king. But before the days of crowns and sceptres, we do not really know how kings were distinguished from other men. The strange rack (*figure 3a*) has been identified as a royal standard; the whetstone (*figure 3c*) as a primitive sceptre. Neither object looks utilitarian; but their functions are frankly unknown. The " standard ", it has even been suggested, may have been a rack for hanging scalps; scalping was a favoured pursuit among the Frankish kings in whose name the Sutton Hoo coins had been issued. It remains true that nothing so magnificent as the Sutton Hoo burial has yet been unearthed; that a fragment of what seems to have been the twin of the helmet at Sutton Hoo has been unearthed in Sweden in a grave generally thought royal—and both are distinctly more magnificent than other Swedish helmets of the time, found in graves presumed non-royal. But there is an element of presumption in this; and we must leave it to the experts to decide. In the meantime we can safely assume that, whether or not the lost warrior was a king, his accoutrements would not have disgraced a king; and if we wish to imagine an early English monarch in state dress, enthroned in his hall, we can clothe him in the trappings of Sutton Hoo.

Nor can we decide the fascinating problem of the absence of his corpse. It has been suggested that he was a Christian, and the spoons, inscribed with St. Paul's two names—Saul, before baptism, and Paul, as a Christian—strongly suggest a christening present, or at least that the warrior had Christian friends. Why, then, the elaborate trappings for his voyage through the afterworld, suitable only to pagan burials? Perhaps the corpse was given Christian burial, while his pagan followers raised a traditional monument to him. Yet this hardly seems likely: it is more probable that the Church tolerated a survival of pagan practices for a space, and allowed a recently converted warrior to be buried in customary style. If the monument was to a pagan king with Christian friends, the likely candidate is Æthelhere of East Anglia, who perished in the battle of *Winwæd* in the north of England in 654, and whose body may have been swept away by a river in flood—which would explain the emptiness of his tomb. If he was a Christian king, the likely candidate was his brother Anna, a far more celebrated man, who died earlier in the year.

The same mingling of pagan and Christian themes puzzles the reader of *Beowulf*. The characters in the poem seem definitely pagan, but the poem itself has a Christian moral and a Christian theme.

The palace of the Danish king is haunted by a monster called Grendel, who visits it nightly and devours such of the warriors as are foolhardy enough to sleep there. The news of this trouble comes to Beowulf, a noble of the " Geats "—the folk of southern Sweden, Gotland or Geatland. Beowulf sets off with a band of followers, and succeeds in killing the monster; he then kills another monster, Grendel's mother, in a fierce encounter at the bottom of a neighbouring lake, and so rids the Danish court of the whole brood. He is feasted by the Danish king and loaded with presents, mostly of gold; and then, to everyone's sorrow, returns to his own people, where he recounts the tale of his adventures to his own king, and passes on to him a share of the gifts. In return for this the Geat king makes Beowulf his closest confidant and loads him with more presents including a large landed estate. So ends the first part of the poem. Years pass: the Geat king and his son are killed, the first in a raid in Friesland in search of booty, the second in a blood feud, and Beowulf has succeeded to the crown—chosen for his suitability by his former master's widow. After years of successful and peaceful rule, his kingdom in its turn is troubled by a monster, in this case by a dragon. The dragon lives on a mound and guards a great treasure which is hidden within the mound; some of the treasure is stolen, and in revenge the dragon lays waste the countryside. Beowulf, now an old man, sets out to save his people from this menace, and kills the dragon; but in the fight he himself receives a mortal wound. The poem concludes with the mourning for his death, and with his burial. He is burnt on a great funeral pyre, and the best horsemen among his followers ride round his pyre, as the Greeks rode round the corpse of Patroclus and the Huns round Attila's.

Beowulf portrays a society of heroic barbarians: courage, prowess in war, loyalty and generosity are the qualities most forcefully portrayed for our admiration. Personal loyalty and kinship are the principal bonds; loyalty above all, for kinship played a less conspicuous part in English society than among the Germanic peoples on the Continent. It is an aristocratic society: a society of chiefs and kings, each with his hall, in which a company of followers can gather. The " following " was the source of a king's power: on his capacity to inspire friends, relations and foreigners to gather round him, on his capacity to lead them successfully in war and to feed and reward them with princely gifts, depended his power and prestige. In *Beowulf* we are given a vision of a barbarian society at its finest.

Yet *Beowulf* is more than that: it is a poem with a specifically Christian moral, applicable to a recently converted barbarian people; first steps in Christian heroism. It is a remarkable fact that Beowulf only kills dragons on the stage, and
hardly any human beings off it. Germanic legends and Germanic history were full of wars and blood-feuds. True heroism does not lie there, says the author of *Beowulf*. But where
does it lie? It may be that Beowulf is a Christian allegory of
a primitive kind, and that the meaning is that true heroism
lies in fighting spiritual enemies, devils, not human beings.
On the surface lies a meaning which would be more likely to
impinge on a warrior audience: " a little less of the blood
feud " was perhaps as much as they would immediately grasp
of its message; and the very existence of the society portrayed
would have been threatened if all the warriors had taken to
fighting dragons or tilting at windmills. The Church had
taken on a tough job when it set about converting the barbarian world; *Beowulf* shows us that it took it seriously, that
it was trying already to devise a notion of Christian heroism; and this ideal may well have appealed to many in its
original audience.

The centre of the story of *Beowulf* is the great hall in which
the Danish king and his followers gather for their evening
banquets, in which the king honours his followers, in which
gifts, and stories, and heroic lays are exchanged. " Such success in arms and so great a fame attended Hrothgar that his
kinsmen were eager to serve under him, and in this way the
number of his young retainers increased until he had a
formidable army. It came into his mind to command the
erection of a building that should be the greatest banqueting
hall ever known, in which he could apportion to young and
old everything that God had entrusted to him, with the exception of public lands and human life. So, as I have heard,
orders were dispatched all over the world for its furbishing;
and in a short time the enormous building was completed.
The king called it Heorot, and kept his promise at the feast,
when he distributed rings and treasure. Tall and wide-

gabled, the hall towered overhead; yet it was to endure
terrible and leaping flames, when in the course of time a
deadly feud between Hrothgar and his son-in-law should be
kindled by an act of violence " (*figure 4a*).

Heorot was large, but simple: an open, barn-like hall,
made of wood. The remains of several such royal halls have
been discovered in England in very recent years: the first,
and most remarkable, at Yeavering, in Northumberland,
where, as has been described, air photography revealed the
traces of a series of buildings, and excavation the foundation
slots and post-holes of several wooden halls. Heorot was of
wood, and in the end caught fire and was burned; and this
probably explains why the palace at Yeavering was several
times replaced. At the time of writing the palace of Saxon
and later kings at Cheddar in Somerset is being excavated;
and a group of buildings covering a wide area has been discovered, at its heart a Saxon timber hall, of the ninth century
or earlier, about 90 ft. by 18 ft. in area.[6]

The halls at Yeavering and Cheddar, like Heorot, were
first and foremost banqueting halls; where a great king or
military leader dined in the evening surrounded by his
followers, the warriors of his " following ", who were bound
to him by the tightest bonds of loyalty. Its magnificence
reflected the king's glory: Heorot, we are told, was plated
with gold. " When we sat down to banquet," Beowulf himself reports, " the king of the Danes rewarded me generously
for this encounter, with treasures and beaten gold. Songs and
junketing followed, and the patriarch Hrothgar, who had a
great fund of stories, told anecdotes about bygone times, and
every now and then played a pleasant melody on the harp.
Now and then some true and unhappy ballad was sung;
occasionally the king would recount a curious legend in its
correct form. . . ." The proceedings were not always orderly.
It was noted as a special sign of virtue in Beowulf that he did
not kill his companions in his cups; and several stories are
told of how feuds were begun or continued by an excited

[6] See the *Observer*, 18 March 1962.

argument, warmed by the potent influence of mead in the
" mead-hall " as it was often called. In spite of such occasional disturbances, the evening was governed by a traditional
order; and closed with a visit from the queen, who carried a
jewelled loving cup round the hall for all to drink; then took
her husband to their chamber for the night. The chamber
was evidently a separate building; and in another separate
building, we are told, Beowulf was lodged when a visitor at the
Danish court. The palace was something like a village, a
group of halls and huts, with the banqueting hall in its midst.
But only the great had separate chambers. Most of the
warriors slept in the hall, including Hrothgar's most trusted
counsellor, who was grabbed from Heorot as he slept by
Grendel's mother. Only the king and specially honoured
guests could expect any privacy.

Heorot was the headquarters of the king and his followers.
From it they went out by day to ride and hunt; in summer,
for longer expeditions, for war, plunder and the pursuit of
feuds; and also to govern their kingdom and do justice. To
Heorot they returned to drink, to exchange gifts, and on more
sober occasions to give counsel.

There is much talk in *Beowulf* of gold. Heorot is plated
with it, the queen adorned with it; the king is an " illustrious
prince and giver of (gold) rings "; every important event is
crowned by the exchange of gifts, in which gold cups and
gold-plated armour are usually conspicuous. This had been
a fundamental part of the life of the barbarian warriors at
the time when the Roman Empire in the west fell to their
arms. Rome supplied them with the bulk of their gold; but
they used it in their own way. They accepted it as the symbol
of wealth and grandeur: a king must be able to display it in
his hall, on his armour, on his wife; he must be able to lavish
gifts of gold on his followers—but yet remain wealthier than
they. This meant a constant scramble to provide themselves
with adequate supplies by loot, by levying tribute, by themselves receiving gifts, and even occasionally, perhaps, by
trade; and it is one of the reasons why plundering expeditions
play so large a part both in the history and the legends of

the fifth and sixth centuries. It helps to explain why the
greatest deposits of Roman gold have been excavated so far
from the Roman Empire—in Scandinavia and the Baltic;
and how treasures from the Mediterranean world, from Gaul
and from Sweden were collected in the grave at Sutton Hoo.

In due course the supply of gold tended to dry up. When
a stable currency was introduced in the eighth century, it was
of silver—as everywhere else in northern Europe by this date.
Even in *Beowulf* there are hints of a more stable basis of
social organisation. The king of the Geats gave Beowulf a
sword whose hilt was covered with gold, but also " a hall and
7,000 hides of land ". This reminds us that land had long
been the most stable form of wealth; that as the supplies of
gold declined it tended to become the regular means of
rewarding a faithful follower. In the English kingdoms the
king was the greatest landowner, and he fed his court either
by wandering from estate to estate eating its produce, or by
arranging for boat- or waggon-loads of produce to be brought
to his halls. In the late seventh century the laws of King Ine
of Wessex give us the following list: " As a food-rent from
10 hides: 10 vats of honey, 300 loaves, 12 'ambers' of
Welsh ale, 30 of clear ale, 2 full-grown cows, or 10 wethers,
10 geese, 20 hens, 10 cheeses, an 'amber' full of butter, 5
salmon, 20 pounds of fodder and 100 eels." This was an
indication, not a precise account; but it reminds us vividly of
the complexity of household management before there was a
stable currency or a proper system of markets or tolerable
conditions of transport. Long before the Norman Conquest,
however, currency and markets had improved beyond King
Ine's imagining; and, even though transport was dismal by
modern standards, it was quite elaborately organised, and the
" farm of one night ", as the basic unit of royal food-rent was
quaintly called, could be translated into cash, into waggon-
loads, that is, of silver pennies. The silver penny was the
only effective currency this country had between its institution
by Offa and the reappearance of a gold coinage in the fourteenth century.

Beowulf gives us a picture of a society of warriors dedicated

to loyal service to their lord, and the faithful pursuit of his
and their own blood-feuds. It is quite clear, however, that
this was not their sole occupation; still less the only concern
of the poem's original audience. Bede describes more than
one Northumbrian king as a man of learning, and to King
Ceolwulf he dedicated his *Ecclesiastical History*. But the
swiftest correction to any notion that Saxon kings were mere
barbarians is a short glance at Asser's *Life* of King Alfred.
No doubt we are in a more humane world than that of
Hengest or Sutton Hoo; we must allow for much growth in
the organisation of the country and the arts of peace. But in
Alfred's time the English kingdoms were threatened with
extinction by the invading armies of the Danes. The *Anglo-
Saxon Chronicle* paints a picture of disaster, and gives the
clear impression that even the victories of Alfred were hard-
won and precarious; even Wessex came near to dissolution.
Alfred, perforce, was a great warrior; nor was he a reluctant
warrior. Asser tells us that he had inherited the tastes of his
kind. He listened eagerly to Saxon poetry day and night—
though we are not told whether this meant epics of heroic
blood-feud, or religious poetry; both kinds were recited in
Heorot, and we may guess that both appealed to Alfred. He
was also passionately fond of the chase, as were all successful
medieval kings: it was the sport of kings; it canalised the
energy of warriors in an occupation less harmful (anyway to
human victims) than war; it accustomed men to swift, rapid
and effective action in the field; it kept them in training.

If this was all we knew of Alfred, we should be excused
for thinking that his life was spent in the hunting field, on
campaign and in the mead-hall; and so he must have spent a
great part of his time. But we also know of a host of other
activities into which he entered with equal ardour. He turned
his penetrating mind to long-term problems of defence, to
improving the fortification of towns, to the design of better
warships, to reorganising the army. He reckoned that a king
must have men who pray and men who work as well as
soldiers, and he cared much for the Church and tried (un-
successfully) to found monasteries. He cared for his estates

and for all his subjects; issued a substantial collection of " laws "; inquired into the activity of law-courts, attempted to raise the standards of his legal officers, constantly interfered. The royal revenue was put on a new footing. Most remarkable of all, he found time for intellectual adventure: organising a seminar of learned men to translate key works of instruction and devotion into English, taking an active part himself in the work of translation; longing to rule a kingdom of literate men—a dream as hopeless, yet inspiring, as so many of his schemes. In the hall at Cheddar Alfred very probably rested from the chase, and dined with his followers like Hrothgar in Heorot; the great hall is the symbol of a militant and military type of kingship. But much else took place in and out of it. Even though Alfred was exceptional, his life reveals what a king could do, the horizons of royal vision; and the variety of his work reminds us that every king had much to do apart from feasting in the mead-hall.

It is also in Alfred's time that we first hear about the workings of the royal treasury and about the king's seal. Royal treasure consisted of jewels, precious metals and coins. Before the Conquest no written accounts were kept, and precious few records of any kind. But by the standards of the day the English treasury was comparatively highly organised: the king and his officers supervised the minting of coin; the king had a variety of sources of revenue which came in due course to include some forms of direct taxation; and it is clear that he could dispose of considerable sums of money. The treasure was normally too bulky for most of it to be carried round, and the late Saxon kings apparently had permanent treasure houses in more than one place, the chief one, no doubt, in Winchester. In the royal chamber, in whatever place the king was staying on his travels, was kept a chest which contained jewels and money for immediate use. The royal secretaries always travelled with the king. The great charters of King Athelstan's time may have been written by royal scribes, or possibly by monks or abbots to whom the task was allotted; and it is doubtful if royal scribes normally wrote royal charters before the time of Athelstan, or in the late tenth and early eleventh centuries. By then, however, the large Latin charter was being replaced by the much smaller " writ ", in origin a letter written in English, as a means for the king to express his royal will. The writ has a special interest, since it was the first serious attempt to make government partly literate, and the first document to which the great seal was attached. We know that Alfred had a seal, but no examples of English royal seals survive before the time of Edward the Confessor. By then it was not uncommon for a royal grant of land or privileges to be written out in a brief writ in English and sent to the court of the shire which it concerned. There a clerk could read the writ to the assembled folk; and although they could not check that he read it aright, since most were illiterate, they could at least see the large lump of wax with the impress of the great seal: it was this which provided the best means of authenticating documents before most men were literate enough to sign their names. In the shire court of Norman times not everyone understood English—French was the language of Norman lords—and so the writ came to conform to the normal convention of written documents in the period, and was written in Latin, to be interpreted no doubt to its audience in whatever languages they understood. But the writ remained the basis of all documents issued under the great seal after the Conquest; in this and in other ways the Normans simply took over and adapted and developed what they found.

The life of the last Saxon king is described idyllically, and naïvely, by his first biographer, writing perhaps while he was still alive: " And so, with the kingdom made safe on all sides by these princes [Earl Harold and his brother], the most kindly King Edward passed his life in security and peace, and spent much of his time in the glades and woods in the pleasures of hunting. After divine service, which he gladly and devoutly attended every day, he took much pleasure in hawks and birds of that kind which they brought before him, and was really delighted by the baying and scrambling of the hounds. In these and such like activities he sometimes spent the day, and it was in these alone that he seemed naturally inclined to snatch some worldly pleasure." The author goes on to say how assiduous Edward was in " practising the Christian religion ", and how he delighted in meeting abbots and monks, especially from overseas. " He used to stand with lamb-like meekness and tranquil mind at the holy offices of the divine mysteries and masses, a worshipper of Christ manifest to all the faithful; and at these times, unless he was addressed, he rarely spoke to anyone "—an unusual virtue apparently; other kings spent the hour of mass in gossip, and Henry I is said to have chosen one of his leading subordinates first of all as his chaplain because he could finish mass in record time. " Moreover, it was quietly, and only for the occasion—in any case, it should be distinctly said, with no mental pleasure—that he displayed the pomp of royal finery in which the queen obligingly arrayed him. And he would not have cared at all if it had been provided at far less cost. He was, however, grateful for the queen's solicitude in these matters, and with a certain kindness of feeling used to remark on her zeal most appreciatively to his intimates. He stooped with great mercy to the poor and infirm, and fully maintained many of these not only daily in his royal court but also at many places in his kingdom. Finally his royal consort did not restrain him in those good works in which he prepared to lead the way, but rather urged speedier progress, and often enough seemed even to lead the way herself. For while he would give now and then, she was prodigal, but aimed her bounty to such good purpose as to consider the highest honour of the king as well. Although by custom and law a royal throne was always prepared for her at the king's side, she preferred, except in church and at the royal table, to sit at his feet, unless perchance he should reach out his hand to her, or with a gesture of the hand invite or command her to sit next to him."

As a picture of a king's life this is clearly one-sided; and although Edward in his later years seems to have been content to leave a part of his work to his subordinates—the army to Harold, the " under-king " as one writer called him, and the administration of government to earls and bishops and sheriffs—this picture of languid sanctity, broken from time to time by a good day's hunting, is probably overdrawn. None the less, it shows us a medieval king in two characteristic places: in the hunting field and in church. The author goes on to describe Edward's zeal for the rebuilding of Westminster Abbey, which he enlarged and re-endowed as a token of his devotion to God and St. Peter, to house his own monument, and, no doubt, to provide a fitting church for the greatest of his palaces. In the second part of the *Life* Edward the king is on the way to becoming Edward the saint—Edward the Confessor: " chosen by God before the day of his birth, and . . . consecrated to the kingdom less by men than . . . by heaven ". God was the real elector; the king was His anointed; and we are told how appropriate this seemed in Edward's case, since God through him performed miracles of healing while he was still alive.

Edward was holy, *sanctus*, in virtue of his office, and also in virtue of his life. The latter claim, first adumbrated in the second part of the *Life*, written shortly after Edward's death, took some time to mature; it was clearly not so obvious to other contemporaries as to the author. Eventually it bore fruit when the monks of Westminster, who possessed the precious relic of his body, with support from Henry II and a throng of leading churchmen, won from Pope Alexander III the bull of canonisation in 1161. Alexander canonised a saint; the monks of Westminster raised a shrine behind their high altar; in popular esteem the sanctity of the royal office was proclaimed. At this date men did not easily distinguish between the king and his office—they were of a piece; loyalty was a personal thing, owed to a man. But in the twelfth century it was argued that a king can do holy things even if he is not holy himself, like a priest.

In the time of William Rufus and Henry I a Norman cleric was deploying some of the most extravagant language ever used about a king to describe the office and person of royalty. The holy chrism transforms a man; makes him the anointed of the Lord, Christ's vicar, his *alter ego*; the holy occupant of a holy office. The Norman Anonymous, at one time known as the "Anonymous of York", here represents old traditional notions of royal authority, the divinity that doth hedge a king, carried to their logical extreme with the help of the tools of the revived logic of the late eleventh century. He also propounded a doctrine which tended to drive a wedge between king and office: the moral authority he ascribes to the king might have seemed fitting in Alfred or Edgar, or even Edward; scarcely in Rufus or Henry I. None the less, the sacral authority of the royal office was widely accepted in Norman times, although rejected, in its more extreme form, by the papacy. The most interesting of Edward's miracles was the first example in England of "touching for the king's evil", the cure of scrofula. Soon after, it became a regular royal practice in France and England; and it seems that this was so already in the days of Henry I—perhaps to emphasise the sacral authority which Henry had inherited by being born after his parents were anointed monarchs, and which he had confirmed by marrying into the line of Cerdic.

The Norman kings were sacred persons, like their predecessors, and they took over much of what they found in every department of kingship. The range of their activities was not much different from that of a Saxon king, though the amount of administrative work organised in their court and household steadily increased; but their dress and the buildings they lived in altered somewhat more. Beowulf, like the lost warrior of Sutton Hoo, was distinguished by his costly armour, especially the helmet, "inlaid with gold, hooped with lordly bands, decorated with effigies of boars". In the Bayeux Tapestry, William and Harold appear in full armour, but they cannot be distinguished from their followers except by the inscriptions: all wear chain-mail, conical helmet with nose-piece, and kite-shaped shield, and carry sword or mace or axe or spear. The crowned helmet, as distinctive royal wear, seems to have come in with Henry I (1100-35). But the Tapestry also shows us Edward and Harold enthroned as kings, with the special royal insignia. The golden helmet was apparently the earliest headgear of Saxon kings; and a jewelled diadem, of late Roman style, appears on early coins.

We do not know when a crown was first worn; it appears on some coins of King Athelstan (925-39), and in a painting of the same king (*figure 6a*). Royal insignia came of age in the coronation of King Edgar in 973. The sceptre was used as well as the crown as a special symbol of kingship—and to it was added soon after the orb—in imitation of Frankish and German monarchs, especially of Otto the Great of Germany, who had been crowned Roman Emperor in 962. Athelstan's crown was a simple ring of metal, with a number of prongs rising from it, plain in shape. By Edgar's time these have blossomed into *fleurs-de-lys*; and the lily-crown is shown in pictures of Edgar, Cnut, Edward the Confessor and Harold. The Conqueror's crown was the work of a Greek craftsman, covered with Arabian gold (so Guy of Amiens tells us) and Egyptian gems; glittering with metal stars and jewels; surmounted by a double bow. In form it may have resembled the Hungarian crown of the eleventh century and perhaps the crown of Otto the Great, which still survives among the imperial treasures in Vienna; it may reveal a conscious imitation by William of the greatness of the German emperors; he shored up his own doubtful claim by increasing still further the outward panoply of kingship.

It is very difficult to reconstruct the palaces of the early Norman kings. No part of the early palaces of Westminster or of Winchester, the most substantial of their many homes, now survives. Perhaps Cheddar, which was still in occupation down to the reign of King John, will show whether the Normans fundamentally altered the style of living of their predecessors. So far as we know, their palaces were not at first much different: a large complex of buildings with a great hall in the centre. The Normans had a passion for raising large buildings of stone; and as time passed, the great aisled hall of timber was replaced by a stone hall, like the beautiful great hall of the castle at Winchester; but this is of the thirteenth century, and is on the site of the castle, not of the old palace.

The stone castle was the characteristic novelty of the Normans. In every large town the Normans built a castle—

many of them held by or in the name of the king; and every Norman baron had his headquarters in one, sometimes several castles. At first these were not usually of stone. But the Conqueror himself set the fashion, which was increasingly followed in the twelfth and thirteenth centuries by leading barons, of building a large castle of stone which could serve both as fortress and house. In most large castles, as in the royal palaces, the main domestic buildings were not part of the fortifications, though they might abut on the inside of the castle walls. But in the enormous keep of the Tower of London (*figure 11b*) built by the Conqueror himself, substantial living rooms were incorporated in the central defensive work of the castle. Apart from cellars, guard rooms and small domestic offices, these great stone keeps normally contained two public rooms, either side by side or one above the other, and a chapel. In the chapel the king or great lord heard mass every morning; and if he were exceptionally devout, other services as well. In the great hall his household lived and ate and slept; in the chamber, a room usually as large or nearly as large as the hall, the king took council and lived withdrawn from the throng, with his family and immediate councillors and servants; and with his jewels and such part of his treasure as he carried with him. The chamber may in some sense have been the king's private apartment; but he had little or no privacy in it. It may well be that king and queen could have more privacy in their larger palaces; and great houses certainly came to have more private rooms in the late Middle Ages. The time when lesser folk expected to have rooms to themselves, when anyone could assume that even the most intimate moments of their life would be spent alone, lay far in the future. Halls and castles were designed for splendour and not for comfort. On great occasions Heorot was adorned with " golden tapestries " and other ornaments, as were many a Norman castle. But its solid furniture consisted merely of benches and tables. When night came the benches were cleared away and " pillows and bedding spread upon the floor ". Things were probably no different in a Norman castle. Tapestries adorned the wall; but there were probably no carpets on the floor; no upholstery on chairs; no glass in the windows. In the twelfth century glass was coming into fashion. But it remained throughout the late Middle Ages a rare extravagance, and the nobleman who possessed a set of windows carried it with him from house to house. As the hall was normally lit and warmed by a great open fire in its midst, the open windows had their advantages; but the Normans never lived without a draught.

Like Edward the Confessor, the Norman kings were all passionately fond of hunting. They added substantially to the area of " forest ", which means, not continuous woodland, but space in which special laws operated, special punishments were enforced, intended to ensure the safe-keeping of game, especially deer and boar. In these areas beasts were more precious than men. It is well known that the early Normans created, or rather extended the New Forest; less well known that they could ride from Windsor, through the New Forest, to the sea without leaving territory subject to the forest laws; that the whole county of Essex was a " forest "; that only three English counties were entirely free from forest law; and that there was probably no part of England more than fifty miles from a forest. William I, says the English chronicler, loved the tall deer as if he were their father.

The life of Edward the Confessor, in his later years, seems to have been relatively peaceful. The Norman kings were rarely at peace with their neighbours, never at peace with themselves. They lived lives of strenuous and hectic activity: hunting, fighting, begetting children, bargaining for advantageous marriages for their children, receiving petitions, taxing their barons, making and enforcing judgement, struggling to enforce a rudimentary order, to foster the country's wealth, founding monasteries, indulging in conventional, sometimes in sensational piety, and in conventional crimes.

Norman kingship was, in a sense, autocratic: there were no strict and precise limits to royal power. The king was expected to consult his councillors, but who were his councillors? When did he have to consult them? on what issues? who could enforce his duty? To these questions there were no simple answers; yet we should be wrong to imagine him free of all restraint on this account, for two good reasons. First, custom might not be precise, but it was deeply felt, and it was supported by oaths made by a king at his accession at least as early as 1066, and sometimes (as in the case of Henry I and Stephen) by a solemn charter extracted from a new king in exchange for his subjects' support and allegiance —a charter which Henry was too strong and Stephen too weak to keep; but Henry I's charter could be unearthed and thrust under the nose of King John on the eve of *Magna Carta*. In the second place, "autocracy" to-day can have instruments to make its will effective. In days before standing armies or regular police forces, with no means of communication faster than a galloping horse, when roads were at best distant memories of Roman ways, at worst "*l'endroit où on passe*", a king had to rely on his people's support if his government was to be effective. England was the most governed country in Europe in the central Middle Ages because it had the most highly developed system of local government. In shire court and hundred court royal officials met the local notables, and they agreed, or agreed to differ, about all the problems of a rudimentary administration. The strength of English local government and its continuity are illustrated by the fact that the boundaries of the English shires were established by the great kings of the tenth century, and then not seriously threatened before the boundary commissions of the twentieth. This does not mean that we should read back democracy into the tenth century, or Parliament into the Witan. The men whom the king had to consult were a small proportion of a population perhaps about three per cent as large as the country holds to-day. This is a rough estimate. The only period in the centuries covered by this book for which we can make anything better than wild guesses of the population of England is in the time of Domesday Book (1086). Even Domesday is no very secure guide. But if we say that there were one and a half million people in England in 1086, and about 200 barons whom the king had to consult, we shall not be far wrong; and we may be fairly sure that in the tenth century the population was smaller, but the Witan somewhat larger. It was only by consulting his leading subjects that the king could hope to rule as well as to reign; only by visiting different parts of the country that he could hope to gain and hold his subjects' loyalty.

Winchester had been the chief city of Wessex for several centuries; London had been the chief city of England even longer—since the Roman conquest, save, perhaps, for an interval after the Romans left. But we should misconceive Saxon or Norman government if we called either the "capital" of England in this period. Government travelled with the king round his many residences; the Witan met where he summoned them. William I held solemn councils at Christmas, Easter and Whitsun; when he was in England these were held at Gloucester, Winchester and Westminster respectively. The kings even carried a proportion of their treasure with them, and the whole of their secretarial staff. It is true that they had permanent treasure-houses here and there; the most important was at Winchester. In the twelfth century it moved, with all the panoply of financial administration, to Westminster. But to the ordinary man kingship meant the person of the king, as he met him on his travels, in the hunting field, in solemn pageant and procession. Where we think of government in terms of Whitehall, Downing Street and the Houses of Parliament, he thought of the royal household.

It is not easy to say precisely in what the royal household consisted in early days; but we are helped by the fact that one of Henry I's clerks drew up a catalogue of the officials of the royal household shortly after his death. This document indicates that the number of household officials was carefully watched, and their wages only paid if they were performing their offices. It is concerned with pay, not with the officers' duties; but it gives the impression that Henry I had had a tight grip on the cost, and on the functions, of his household. None the less, it presupposes a household of at least 100, and possibly far more persons in regular employment, ranging from the heads of the departments, whose wages were 5s. per day, to the laundress, whose wages could not be discovered. The chancellor was head of the chapel and the writing office (oddly enough, as we see it, the same department); two "sewers" or stewards, called "cupbearers", *dapiferi*, were in charge of the pantry and the kitchen; the butler had charge of buttery and cellar; the master chamberlain and treasurer between them controlled the royal chamber, the royal treasury, and the recently formed audit department, the exchequer; the constables looked after the royal army and the king's horses. The chancellor was usually a leading cleric, likely to be rewarded sooner or later with a bishopric; the treasurer was sometimes a cleric, sometimes a layman; the other heads of departments were all leading barons, ministers of state of a rudimentary kind. The butler performed the ceremonial work of his office indeed; but he was in no sense a menial. Each of these great men had a staff of subordinates, who did the real work of their offices. The largest of all the departments, characteristically, was that of the hunting staff: four horn-blowers, twenty sergeants, sundry keepers of greyhounds, keepers of the royal pack, knight-huntsmen, ordinary huntsmen, a leader and a feeder of the hounds, huntsmen of the "trained pack" (hounds kept on a long lead), the keeper of the small hounds, wolf-hunters, archers.

The court was mobile; the household included a tent-keeper for the royal pavilion. It was large, but had to be prepared for frequent and exhausting travel on horse-back, with a train of ox-drawn and horse-drawn waggons and pack-horses. It was the centre of government: the chancery, the royal jewels and a part of the royal treasure travelled with it, only the treasury and exchequer were static in Winchester. It was the magnificent household of a great lord whose splendour must impress his visitors; it was also a domestic organisation with chamber, pantry, buttery and kitchen. It was the head-quarters of a war-lord, with constables and marshals to organise the troops. But as one's eyes wander to and fro through the pages of the catalogue, ever and anon they return to the final item: the hunting staff. It reminds us that the consuming occupation of medieval kings was hunting; it is the monument of a savage sport in which men and animals were sacrificed to delight in an adventure often more destructive than medieval war; compared with which hunting to-day —under the constant supervision of the Anti-Blood Sports League—is a comparatively humane affair. It is also the personal monument of a man who won a kingdom in the hunting field.

CHAPTER IV

ORIGINS

Such, in broad outline, were the institutions of Saxon and Norman kingship. Now we can turn and pursue the fascinating problem of its origin. In doing so, we must keep a firm grip on ourselves; pursue real clues, proceed by paths that are, or can be, mapped; avoid the wild speculations to which such subjects are always inviting us.

In this pursuit we can get some guidance from the studies of social anthropologists. They have studied the institutions of modern peoples in a variety of states from savagery, through barbarism to civilisation, many with highly developed ideas of kingship, many with none at all. They warn us that kingship is not a " natural " or " inevitable " feature of any type of society, but show that some sort of kingship has been very common in many different parts of the world. Clearly it answers some widely felt needs of human society; precisely how is not easy, in a general way, to say. Most kingships have had a religious and a military significance; we shall do well to look at Anglo-Saxon warfare and religion at an early stage.

The chief lesson of modern anthropology seems to be a warning of our ignorance. When modern, illiterate societies were first examined by scientific methods, attempts were made to deduce the historical evolution of their arrangements, partly by using certain assumptions about how societies work, partly by deductions from the oral traditions of the peoples themselves. The technique of deducing history in this way is now discredited: it produced much fascinating speculation, often contradictory. The anthropologist now studies the structure, the functioning of a society as he sees it; and, if he talks history, it is " structural history ", that is to say he constructs a model, in terms of two or three generations, of how the existing society works. Thus he is able to clarify, and rationalise, the data of present experience; and also to make sense of the people's oral " history ". Oral history may often contain fragments of genuine tradition going back many centuries; in extreme cases these fragments may hardly alter through the generations; but oral history as we find it to-day is a compound of old traditions and new; of stories genuine and garbled; and it is intended to explain the present—as a crude attempt in its own right at " structural history "—not a self-conscious attempt to describe the past for its own sake. By merely inspecting current oral tradition we can never hope to distinguish old from new with any precision; we can only prove the presence of the old if earlier written records or archæological finds confirm it. This helps to explain why genuine traditions of widely different centuries may become mingled together. The sense of time, as a thing of centuries and decades, is a very sophisticated notion; to most people, especially primitive people, a thousand years are as yesterday, or at least, as the day before yesterday. Students of medieval sources are constantly baffled by the way that plausible history and the wildest fantasy are so often set down side by side, as if of equal credibility. This is partly due to the fact that the medieval world of experience was different from ours—was peopled with devils and monsters and strange, miraculous prodigies, which tend to evade us; partly because only a few men had any concrete notion of the past. A historian like Bede could set seriously to work to piece his materials together into a coherent historical narrative; but he was a rare and startling exception. To most men the past only existed in so far as they or their friends could remember it; and was only recorded in so far as it intrigued them or helped to explain the present.

An extreme example is the practice, common in the modern world as in the medieval, of recording a man's genealogy. The study of genealogy among primitive peoples, as practised by the modern anthropologist, is a highly technical and refined art. The genealogy exists, among other things, to establish a man's title to land, to record his relationship to the tribe or people who own the whole country in which he lives. If it achieves this task, it matters little whether it represents genuine relationships or not. Indeed, in those societies where the rules of inheritance are very complex, and where patrilineal succession is unknown, a genealogy clearly does not represent a family tree of the kind to which we are accustomed. The early Anglo-Saxon genealogies purport to establish the succession to kingdoms, and may contain some genuine king-lists; they may also contain some fiction; they are less likely to give a true account of a man's ancestry. But in some cases, as we shall see, even this is not wholly impossible.

Modern anthropology warns us of our ignorance in another, even more fundamental way. Its students rely on living material; like the psychologist, they can analyse their material, ask it what questions they like, study its reactions to problems of their own choosing. They would not describe a society or a type of kingship which they had not subjected to these tests. The historian has the advantage of studying his victims in depth; but their structure, as the anthropologist understands the term, he cannot study at all. He can find the footprint of Man Friday in the sand; but he cannot meet Man Friday face to face.

" His genealogy ", wrote Asser of King Alfred (871-99), " is woven in this order: Alfred " was the son of Æthelwulf, son of Egbert, son of Ealhmund, son of Eafa, son of Eoppa, son of Ingild; Ingild and Ine were brothers, sons of Cenred, son of Ceolwald, son of Cutha (Cuthwulf), son of Cuthwine, son of Ceawlin, son of Cynric, son of Creoda, son of Cerdic, son of Elesa, son of Gewis, son of Brond, son of Bældæg, son of Woden, son of Frithuwald, son of Frealaf, son of Frithuwulf, son of Finn, son of Godwulf, son of Geat (whom " the pagans long venerated as a god "), son of Tætwa, son of Beaw, son of Sceldwea, son of Heremod, son of Itermon, son of Hathra, son of Hwala, son of Bedwig, son of Seth, son of Noah, son of Lamech, son of Methuselah, son of Enoch, son of Malaleel, son of Canaan, son of Enos, son of Seth, son of Adam.

This list lacks nothing in completeness; the greater part of it, none the less, was the fruit of recent speculation. In the early ninth century it was firmly believed that the West Saxon kings were descended from Cerdic; it was equally firmly believed, needless to say, that they were also descended from Adam. The vital links in the chain between Cerdic and Adam were Woden, Geat and Seth. These links were all forged in the early or mid-ninth century. The kings of almost all Saxon kingdoms claimed to be descended from Woden. Oddly enough, the West Saxons seem in early days not to have looked back beyond Cerdic. This defect was now made good: a section from one of the Northumbrian genealogies, that of Bernicia, was added, and so Cerdic was linked to Woden; and Woden became the common ancestor of the West Saxon, and nearly all the Saxon lines.

Woden had been the high god of the Teutonic pantheon, the leader of the Germanic peoples—though his position had been disputed by Thor. His name survives in place-names like Wednesbury and Wednesfield, and also in the English translation of the Latin *dies Mercurii* "Mercury's day", Wednesday (French *mercredi*), just as Thursday is Thor's day (Jupiter's day, *jeudi*). The idea that kings ought to be descended from him was very ancient; but originally he himself had no ancestors. It seems to have been the royal minstrels of the obscure kingdom of Lindsey (in Lincolnshire) who bolstered up the decaying authority of their masters by pushing back their ancestry some generations behind Woden, as far as Geat, and this became part of the accepted lore of English royal descent. The next stage is somewhat obscure. But it seems that Geat was presently identified with another legendary figure of the same name, whose ancestors were already recorded; and this enabled the genealogy of all the Saxon houses to be extended to one "Sceaf", perhaps originally the same as the Sceaf whose son Scyld's ship-burial formed the start of *Beowulf*. According to *Beowulf* Scyld was put into a ship when he was dead; it also says, as do other early traditions, that he began his career in a ship. By what mysterious alchemy his father was made a son of

Noah and brought to birth, as it were, in the Ark, is far from clear; but by the time we get to Asser he has been given a Hebrew name, Seth, and is performing the genealogical function of Japhet. From then on, all was plain sailing.

If we look closely at Alfred's genealogy, we can see that his folk had no ancient tradition of their ancestry going behind Cerdic. It is striking that the Saxon line which was ultimately to give England her kings had the shortest and most confused of early traditions. All the kings from Cerdic to Cenred, Ine's father, begin with C. It may be that this alliteration was an established tradition: all Ine's successors to Edgar the Ætheling began with a vowel. But it is unlikely that the succession was so orderly as this assumes; it is striking that the change from initial " C " to vowels comes just where the line emerges into the plain light of day; and although some of the line were undoubtedly historical, it is likely that some names have been added from the medieval equivalent of a telephone directory, and that it is in part fictitious. Oddest of all, the founder seems not to have been a Saxon at all: his name, Cerdic, or Ceredig, is Welsh.

Let us put on one side the mystery of Wessex for the time being, and see why historians, without undue credulity, have greater faith in others of the genealogies. Most remarkable of all is the list for Lindsey which is to all intents and purposes our only evidence for the history of that kingdom. It lay neglected until Sir Frank Stenton, in a brilliant article, showed how it could be made to illuminate the history of its kingdom and of England at large. Ten names take us to Woden, and not one of them can be certainly identified; nor does Woden give us any very secure chronological beginning, still less the mysterious names which carry us beyond him. But Sir Frank noted four remarkable things about the list: that it is undoubtedly early since it contains early Saxon names which later fell out of use—like the name next to Woden, Winta, preserved in no document, but known from early place-names to have existed; that the fourth name from Woden revealed Celtic influence—i.e. belonged to a time when the two races had mingled; that the seventh,

Biscop (= Bishop) revealed Christian influence, and must belong after the conversion of Lindsey, that is, to the seventh century at earliest; and that the tenth and latest, Aldfrith, bore the same name as an unidentified king in a South Saxon charter of the time of Offa of Mercia. By a process of elimination the identification of the two kings is made very probable; and this explains why the genealogy ends with Aldfrith—the minor Anglian dynasties did not for the most part survive the supremacy of Mercia. There is thus every possibility that the genealogy of Lindsey is genuine, or at least a genuine list of kings. We may add that, if one counts the generations back to Winta, it would seem that the dynasty began towards the end of the fifth century. This is a very hazardous means of calculation, but it suggests that Winta may have been the first king of Lindsey, not, like the founder of the Mercian house, a continental Angle.

Various pieces of evidence make the Mercian genealogy seem one of the oldest that survive; and at a point which would seem (by counting generations) to fall approximately in the late fourth century there occurs the name of Offa, who played a part in early legend almost as outstanding as his great namesake of the eighth century played in Mercian and English history. Offa of Mercia seems in fact to have been descended from a continental Angle of the same name who flourished a century before the Saxons came to England.

All discussions of German kingship come back in the end to a terse sentence in the *Germania* of Tacitus (1st century A.D.), a slender foundation on which many large buildings have been erected: " kings they choose on grounds of noble ancestry; war-leaders for their courage ": *reges ex nobilitate, duces ex virtute sumunt.* It is clear that many successful *duces* became kings in course of time; and for some of these noble ancestry was invented. But it may well be that the founders of Lindsey and Mercia were *reges*, just as we can be fairly sure that Cerdic was a *dux*—a Welsh soldier of fortune who became a Saxon war-leader, perhaps; and if this collocation sounds strangely in our ears, let us remember that in the fifth century Romans were sometimes found in the employment of Goths and Huns, and a Hun, Odoacer, became effective ruler of Rome.

Beyond this, I doubt if the modern study of genealogy can help us. It warns us to look for fiction in the midst of fact, and fact in the midst of fiction; and it also warns us to look for an explanation of the original form of a genealogy in terms of the social organisation of the tribe to which it belongs. But this final warning does us no good: we do not know the form taken by any of these genealogies before the eighth century; and we know too little of the social organisation of the Anglo-Saxons to be sure how it would affect their genealogies.

The word "king" is common to all known Germanic languages, and it seems that all Germanic people enjoyed the institution at one time or another. H. M. Chadwick believed that the word meant originally "son of the family", emphasising that kings came "*ex nobilitate*". But surviving evidence does not permit us to discuss the nature of "Germanic kingship" in general terms at all. When Goths and Vandals and Lombards emerged on to the stage of history, they had strong, unified monarchies; the kings frequently claimed to be derived from the best ancient stock, but in fact, as the conditions of the barbarian invasions dictated, "*virtus*" mattered more to them than "*nobilitas*"; "election" than "heredity". In a new land the absence of nobility was more easily forgotten than in the old. The Byzantine historian Procopius tells a wonderfully absurd story about one small German tribe, the Heruli. They decided to abolish kingship and killed their king; then changed their mind, and sent to Scandinavia in search of a scion of the old royal family; then changed their minds again and asked the Emperor Justinian to provide them with a king; and finally, when the prince from Scandinavia arrived, changed their minds a third time, and accepted him. The Goths looked to the Romans, not for a king, but to provide a genealogy for one already established. These stories illustrate the variety of possibility open to a German tribe; they tell us little of the "origin" of Germanic kingship, and we shall search for it in vain.

Across the Channel in France, to be more precise in Merovingian Gaul, there flourished a German kingdom which more closely resembled those of the Anglo-Saxons. The Franks invaded Gaul in the fifth century from the Rhineland; and conquered most of what we call France under the first of their great kings, the celebrated Clovis. Clovis began his career as one petty king among many; the exigencies and opportunities of conquest, and a total absence of scruple which is delightfully portrayed in the pages of Gregory of Tours' *History of the Franks*, enabled Clovis to unite the whole Frankish people under a single rule, for the first time in recorded history. But to the Franks kingship did not traditionally mean " monarchy ", which literally means the rule of one man. A kingdom was divided between the sons of a ruler, and so the sons of Clovis split Francia between them. They were kings *ex nobilitate*; they were " Merovingians ", heirs of Clovis and his distant predecessor " Meroving ", and in later times at least symbolised the special nature of their descent by wearing their hair longer than was fashionable. So efficacious was their long hair, that it kept the last of the Merovings on the throne long after he had ceased to wield any real power; the dynasty did not disappear until 751. Meanwhile there was sometimes one, sometimes a whole committee of kings. In earlier times they may have ruled jointly, like the kings in *The Gondoliers*; in later times they divided the kingdom between them. The early Merovingians were noted for their violence, rapacity and cunning, even in a Europe well acquainted with these qualities; and accident and assassination from time to time left a single king in charge of the whole kingdom. But the principle of family inheritance never disappeared, and " election " was never more than a formality—the formality of raising a new king on the shield, of acknowledging him as a leader.

In England almost every king from Hengest to Edward the Confessor claimed to be of royal descent. When Northumbria was threatened with destruction by the Danes, its people in despair elected the non-royal Ælla as the last of their kings; the Mercians probably also took a non-royal king in Ceolwulf

II under the same disastrous pressure. The only other example known was Harold II himself. As we have seen, the principle of heredity, and of primogeniture, with certain notable qualifications, was firmly established. But in early days it seems that the English kings, like the Frankish, were not " monarchs "; and it may even be that whole families of sons, brothers and even nephews of kings were called " kings ". When Edwin of Northumbria invaded Wessex, he killed five West Saxon kings in one battle. In many cases, perhaps in most, the committee had a chairman: the senior king had ultimate authority. But in some, even in the seventh and eighth centuries, the kings were equal, like Sigehere and Sebbe of East Anglia. This principle of joint-kingship goes back as far as our records: according to the *Anglo-Saxon Chronicle* the brothers Hengest and Horsa were joint-kings of Kent, and when Horsa died Aesc, Hengest's son, took his place. The same source makes Cerdic and Cynric, his son, joint-kings of the West Saxons; and the examples could be multiplied. In both these cases there may well be an element of anachronism, and even of fiction. But they imply clearly that kingship was not thought of as rule by one man: we have no record of a time when Anglo-Saxon kings had been monarchs.

Even *The Gondoliers* ends with the restoration of monarchy; and in many countries and tribes in the early Middle Ages in which kingship was divided or kings were three a penny, there was some inkling of the possibility of unified monarchy. Ireland had its high king; the Franks commonly regarded one of their kings as the senior; the English had their " Bretwaldas ".

The word *Bretwalda* probably means " ruler of Britain ". The title was clearly echoed later in the title used on his coins by King Athelstan in the tenth century: " *rex totius Britannie* ", king of all Britain. Perhaps we should not take this title too seriously: it was apparently copied shortly after his death by a swashbuckling pirate called Anlaf, the Irish-Norse king of York. Athelstan could only claim effective rule in England, and the title " king of the English ", already used by Alfred on his coins (alternately with "king of the Saxons"), was the one ultimately adopted by their successors, true kings of a united England. But Athelstan's title was not pure fantasy. Scottish and Welsh kings admitted his over-lordship; he was widely respected outside the mainland of Britain. There is some reason to think that he used the title "emperor", as did the kings of León in northern Spain in the tenth century, on account of the many peoples he ruled over or might claim to rule. It is unlikely that he had any wish to forestall his brother-in-law, Otto the Great of Germany, who some years after Athelstan's death was crowned "Roman" emperor in Rome. But he occasionally used the title "Basileus", the official title of the Eastern Roman, or Byzantine Emperor; and "*Anglorum Basileus*" is the style of Edward the Confessor on the earliest surviving impressions of the Great Seal of England.

If we inquire why Athelstan appeared on his coins as king of the whole of Britain, the likely answer is that he was recalling the proud title of his great-great-grandfather Egbert, the last of the *Bretwaldas*. In 829 "King Egbert conquered Mercia, and all that was south of the Humber, and he was the eighth king to be *Bretwalda*: the first to rule so great a kingdom was Ælle, king of Sussex; the second was Ceawlin, king of Wessex; the third was Ethelbert, king of Kent; the fourth was Rædwald, king of East Anglia; the fifth was Edwin, king of Northumbria; the sixth was Oswald who reigned after him; the seventh was Oswiu, Oswald's brother; the eighth was Egbert, king of Wessex. This Egbert led his levies to Dore against the Northumbrians, where they offered him submission and peace; thereupon they parted." The same list, with the omission of Egbert, occurs in Bede over a century earlier. It is a very interesting, and in some ways a very strange, selection. But before we can attempt to understand the selection, or understand what made a man a *Bretwalda*, we must tell in outline the story of the English kingdoms between Hengest and Egbert.

CHAPTER V

THE SMALL KINGDOMS

The map of England is a palimpsest on which every age has scored its marks; and time, an incompetent eraser, has left much for our inspection. It is a curious fact that the English shire boundaries were fixed before the boundary with Scotland: all the shires we know, with almost exactly their modern boundaries, were established by the end of the tenth century, save only the four northern counties and Rutland. The shires represent the administrative skill of the tenth-century kings; but there is much earlier history incorporated in them. Among those of the south-east, Kent and Sussex and Essex were ancient kingdoms, long since absorbed into larger units; Norfolk and Suffolk had long been joined in East Anglia, a kingdom which had flourished in the seventh century, and survived until the ninth. The shires of the east midlands were carved out of the later kingdoms of the northern Danelaw, the area conquered and settled by the Danes in the ninth and tenth centuries, and they combine Danish elements and earlier groupings. Some shires were grouped round four of the " five boroughs ", the Danish capitals in the east midlands, Derby, Leicester, Lincoln and Nottingham. Lincolnshire still included the old kingdom of Lindsey; but like Yorkshire, based on the ancient kingdom of Deira, it was divided by the Vikings into three ridings (as one might say "thirdings "). Further north, the later county of Northumberland was to enshrine the name of the English kingdom of Northumbria, which before the coming of the Danes had stretched from the Forth to the Humber, including Deira (modern Yorkshire) and Bernicia (Northumberland and Durham and south-eastern Scotland); it had also included great stretches of north-western England.

The shires of the west midlands were artificially created by the tenth-century kings out of the old kingdom of Mercia.

The earlier units are represented not by county boundaries, but by the boundaries of the medieval dioceses of Lichfield-Coventry (Mercia proper), Hereford (the Magonsæte) and Worcester (the Hwicce). The Magonsæte and Hwicce were representatives of the very numerous peoples and small kingdoms which were in due course absorbed into the larger kingdoms of later Saxon times. Many of these, like the Middle Angles, who were among the predecessors of the Mercians, or the Gewissae, who were the predecessors of the West Saxons (or folk of Wessex), have left almost no mark on the map of England. Others, less important in their day, have left as clear an imprint as any so far mentioned; for the counties in the west of Wessex grew out of the little Celtic principalities of Cornwall and Devon, the last Celtic parts of England to be conquered. The other counties of Wessex were divisions made at a date much earlier than the tenth century: Dorset was the shire of the *Dorsætan,* the folk administered from Dorchester, Somerset of the *Somersætan,* the folk administered from Somerton; Wiltshire was the shire of the folk administered from Wilton, Hampshire of the folk administered from Southampton. The earlier, pre-West Saxon, groupings have disappeared.

Before the Danish invasions most of the country had been ruled for two hundred years or more by the kings of Northumbria, Mercia and Wessex; and because the kings of East Anglia, Essex, Kent and Sussex were still something more than an antiquarian memory, the seventh and eighth centuries used to be known as the period of the " heptarchy ", the seven kingdoms, although in the constantly shifting sands there were almost always more or less than seven kings in England. In 450 there were no Saxon kingdoms in this island; in the next 250 years a multiplicity were formed; by 700 the three giants, with a variable group of satellites, were firmly established. Our problem now is to penetrate behind the year 700 and see how these kingdoms had been formed.

Their names fall into two groups: some are Saxon in form, some pre-Saxon. Bernicia and Deira are Celtic words; their history can be traced back to the sixth century, but their

THE ENGLISH KINGDOMS

The boundaries are approximately those of the eighth century: by
the end of the century only the kingdoms named in capital letters
retained any real independence. But kingdoms and their frontiers
were always changing—the frontier of Northumbria too frequently
for it to be possible to show it on this map.

origin is a mystery. Kent is also a Celtic name; it was known as *Cantium* in Cæsar's time. All these seem to represent earlier units revived by Saxon war-lords. Lindsey is a hybrid: the island surrounding the old Roman town of Lincoln (*Lindum*). In the course of the seventh century a pattern of Saxon names was spread over the other parts of England. These names were based on the assumption that the people of the south were Saxons, the people of the north Angles—i.e. that the south was colonised from north-western Germany, the north from southern Denmark and the parts of Germany adjacent to it. Thus the southern divisions were those of the West, Middle, South and East Saxons—Wessex, Middlesex, Sussex and Essex; the middle kingdoms were those of the East and Middle Angles, and of the Mercians, the Angles of the " march ", the frontier, presumably (though not quite certainly) of Wales. This division of Saxons and Angles was canonised in a famous passage in Bede, which also speaks of the " Jutes " from Jutland, who are supposed to have colonised Kent and Hampshire. But the Jutes are a very obscure people. Bede thought that they came from Jutland on account of their name; but it seems they came from Friesland and the Rhineland and not from Jutland; and they have left no clear mark on the map. Bede also adds that all the folk north of the Humber (a part of the area of the Angles) were called " Northumbrians ". Bede intended his book to be read by others than Englishmen; and so he explains some pieces of geography—such as the situation of Ireland— which would hardly need explaining to an educated Englishman. But he glosses " Northumbrians " as " those who live north of the Humber " no less than three times, which seems to establish that the name was novel, and not yet generally familiar, and has even been taken as evidence that Bede himself invented it.

As we move back from Bede's day, the early eighth century, these highly rational tribal names gradually dissolve. Northumbria breaks up into Bernicia and Deira, first united in the late sixth century; Mercia dissolves as we look into the early seventh century; Wessex also changes its name and shape as we look into the seventh century. These names are artificial creations of leading kings of the sixth and seventh centuries, and we cannot tell their story in detail, but in outline it is likely that it went something like this.

In the mid-fifth century, perhaps under the leadership of Hengest and Horsa, the Saxons first established settlements of their own. They encouraged others to follow them, and from all along the littoral of North Germany and Denmark settlers came. They pressed up the navigable rivers, and the Humber, the Wash and the Thames became their chief centres of communication. The method of their settlement—by flotillas of ships—tended to break up the old social and tribal groupings from which they came. "Kinship" was more easily and rapidly forgotten than among the continental Germans. They remembered the land of their origin; but the various peoples evidently mingled in all parts of conquered England. To outsiders they were known, indifferently, as Angles or Saxons. Some of the leaders were new men, thrown up by the opportunities of the invasion; leaders of motley bands, they may well have cared little for whether they were Angles, Saxons or "Jutes". They were happy to make use of existing names for their kingdoms. But some of the leaders were not new men; and some leaders, from families old or new, no doubt cared much for the history of their race before it crossed the sea, and some maintained communication with the homeland.

In the late fifth century a powerful leader called Ælle established a kingdom in what we call Sussex; and he or one of his successors proudly called his people the "South Saxons", having absorbed the earlier unit of "Hæsta's folk", *Hæstingas*, whose name survives in Hastings. At the turn of the sixth and seventh centuries a great king arose in Norfolk and Suffolk; and Rædwald was duly acclaimed king of the East Angles. He may have been the first to have the title; it can hardly have existed more than a generation or so before his birth. In the sixth century the Angles of the midlands came to be dominated by the rulers of Middle Anglia and Mercia, and they claimed descent from the mighty Offa, king of the continental Angles, and made quite sure they were Angles and not Saxons; and it may well be to this dynasty that we owe the final imprint of this pattern on English geography. The dynasty of Mercia may have been kings or warlords from the earliest days of the conquest; but if so it is clear that they did not rule Mercia then, or only a fragment of it. Similarly there may well have been some continuity in other families, but it was a continuity of lordship, not of a kingdom of defined boundaries. Sussex and the kingdoms of Celtic title—Bernicia, Deira, Lindsey, Kent—had long, continuous histories, perhaps going back into the fifth century, though in no case is this certain. Kent may even claim to go right back to the first dawn of conquest; but some scholars now doubt whether Hengest really operated in Kent.

The history of the kingdoms and dynasties is illustrated most clearly from the family of Cerdic. Cerdic was an ealdorman,[7] a *dux*—presumably, in fact, an adventurer—whose military prowess enabled him to found the greatest dynasty of all. His name is Celtic, and it is possible that he was himself of Celtic birth, or the son of a Celt who had joined the English insurgents—an event not uncommon in the confusion of the barbarian invasions; and it may be significant that he won his successes just at the time when the Britons were staging a revival, and driving the English from much of the midlands. But he appears on the scene as a Saxon leader, and his descendants bore Saxon names. In 495 and later he is said by the *Anglo-Saxon Chronicle* to have conquered parts of the south coast and the Isle of Wight from the Britons. About 500 occurred the famous battle of *Mons Badonicus*, in which, according to tradition, Arthur led a British confedera-

---

[7] " Ealdorman " was the highest title of the Anglo-Saxon nobility under the king, and was later replaced by the Danish " jarl " or earl. In this case it apparently means a military leader who was not of royal birth. The dates in this part of the *Chronicle* are not at all reliable, and one wonders in particular whether it is true that Cerdic died in 534 and his great-grandson rose to power in 560. It is possible: but we cannot be sure that either the relationship or Cerdic's dates are correctly recorded. 495 is very probably too early; 534 may be too late.

tion to victory over the Saxons; and there is little doubt that for two generations or so the midlands were British once more. This did not prevent Cerdic from carving out his principality in the south. But the greatness of his family probably owed more to Ceawlin, traditionally Cerdic's great-grandson, who about 560 organised a confederation which in the course of the next thirty years drove the Britons out of the south midlands and outbid all Saxon rivals in southern England. His people were known as the *Gewissae*, and although later speculators invented one Gewis, grandfather to Cerdic, to explain the name, it is highly probable that it really meant "the confederates"; for confederates they un-doubtedly were, as, in origin, were all barbarian tribes and kingdoms large enough to embark on a career of conquest. Sometimes these confederations lasted, and gave their names to later and more stable political units; sometimes they were ephemeral. The *Gewissae*, in a sense, were both.

In the course of the seventh century the Mercian power in the midlands grew at the expense of all its neighbours; and in due course the *Gewissae* were driven from the upper Thames valley, the centre of Ceawlin's power, and confined to the south. Meanwhile they were compensating themselves in the south-west, driving the Britons out of Somerset, later conquering Devon and ultimately Cornwall too. The most notable of their kings in this period, Cædwalla (685-8) and Ine (688-726), showed their standards in Kent and Sussex; but their own kingdom was now definitely defined as south-western England; and as the new political geography of the age became established, and the power of Cædwalla and Ine stabilised, they became generally known as kings of the "West Saxons". The name *Gewissae* remained as an anti-quarian memory, but thenceforth Cerdic's descendants called themselves kings of the West Saxons; their kingdom lasted until it came to absorb the whole of England, and its memory was canonised by Thomas Hardy. Hardy's Wessex was smaller than Alfred's; but its core was the true core of Ine's power: Dorset, Wiltshire and Hampshire.

Cædwalla was a member of a cadet branch of the house of

Cerdic; or so he claimed. All that we can assert with confidence is that he bore a British name, equivalent to " Cadwallon ", the name of the greatest Welsh king of the preceding generation, and that he was a successful adventurer. After an abortive attempt to carve out a principality in Sussex, he won the Gewissan throne in 685; spent three years in warfare, loot and arson in Kent, Sussex, Surrey and the Isle of Wight, and then, with dramatic suddenness, abandoned his kingdom and went on pilgrimage to Rome. He was still young, but evidently had suffered in the fighting and realised that his end was not far off. He was both a barbarian and a Christian; he knew his career in the first role was drawing to a close, and so he hastily embarked on the second before it was too late; went to Rome; was baptised and given the name " Peter " by the pope; and died, in the white robes of baptism, on 20 April 689. His dramatic career and edifying end made a deep impression on contemporaries, and Bede devotes more space to Cædwalla's three years than to his successor's thirty-seven—he says little more than that Ine, at the end of his long reign, followed Cædwalla's example, withdrew to Rome and died there. But it is clear that Ine had a far deeper influence on the West Saxon kingdom, and was one of the most distinguished of Alfred's predecessors. The *Chronicle* tells us of occasional outbreaks of violence, and little besides. But his foundation of a new see at Sherborne, whose first bishop was the famous St. Aldhelm, and his benefactions to Glastonbury Abbey, reveal a real interest in the Church and an attempt to weld together the Celtic and Saxon elements in his kingdom; Sherborne was the first see specifically for the west of Wessex, in Glastonbury Saxon and Celtic Christianity met and mingled, in Aldhelm was represented the learning both of Ireland and of Europe. Ine's laws, furthermore, are the most substantial early code to survive; significantly, they owe their survival to Alfred, for they show the same passionate concern to establish some semblance of order in an unruly kingdom and the same sense that earthly laws are subject to the divine law which marks Alfred's own.

" I, Ine, by the grace of God, king of the West Saxons,"

runs the prologue, " with the advice and with the instruction of my father Cenred, and my bishop Hædde [of Winchester], and my bishop Eorcenwold [of London], along with all my ealdormen and the chief councillors of my people, and also a great assembly of the servants of God, have been inquiring about the salvation of our souls and about the security of our kingdom, that true law and true statutes might be established and strengthened throughout our people, so that none of the ealdormen or of our subjects might afterwards pervert these our decrees."

Powerful as Ine was, he was not reckoned among the greatest of English kings by his contemporaries or immediate successors. When the *Chronicle* records the conquest of Mercia by King Egbert of Wessex in 829, it lists the *Bret-waldas* who had preceded him. The list, in fact, is identical with that given by Bede a century earlier: Ælle king of Sussex, Ceawlin of " Wessex ", Ethelbert of Kent, Rædwald of East Anglia, Edwin, Oswiu and Oswald of Northumbria. In early days a single kingdom might have several kings; but one was usually recognised as the chief ruler; and, although the whole of England was never united before the tenth or eleventh century, from time to time a ruler arose whose suzerainty was recognised over a great part of England, and sometimes over parts of Wales and Scotland too. His rule was personal, and depended on his prestige as a successful warrior; usually it died with him. He was called *Bretwalda*, ruler, not of England, but of Britain. This title seems to be ancient, is perhaps a memory of titles held by British princes like Vortigern before the coming of the Saxons. It was clearly a title of great prestige; equally clearly, it was not an institution, it carried no formal rights with it.

We owe the list to Bede, and it has many odd features. The title seems to have assumed lordship of some kind over a substantial proportion of England, especially of England south of the Humber; and this would explain why Ine is omitted. But there is no reason to suppose that Ælle ruled any people save the South Saxons; and it is difficult to know how widely spread was the power of Ceawlin, Ethelbert or

Rædwald. If these names deserved a place, did not the makers of the Mercian kingdom also, and especially Penda (died 654) and Wulfhere (died 674)? Still more, when the list was brought up to date in the ninth century, how did it come to omit the greatest of the Mercians, Ethelbald and Offa, whose rule extended over almost the whole of England? In this we can certainly detect the operation of prejudice. Ethelbald and Offa used the title " king of Britain " in their charters, and certainly regarded themselves as *Bretwaldas*. Penda was a pagan, one of the most considerable pagan rulers of the seventh century, and might have been excluded on this score. But Ælle, Ceawlin and Rædwald were also pagans, and Bede may here reflect a Northumbrian prejudice against the Mercians, as the *Chronicle* undoubtedly reflects West Saxon prejudice against the Mercians in omitting Ethelbald and Offa.

One striking feature of Bede's list is that, if one omits the first name, it is almost continuous. One cannot be very precise about this, since a man was only regarded as *Bretwalda* while his supremacy was effective, and in several cases we do not know how long this lasted. But if we reflect that Ceawlin flourished from 560 to 591, that Ethelbert was king of Kent from 560 to 616 and presumably *Bretwalda* in the 590's, that Rædwald was already *Bretwalda* before Ethelbert's death and himself died about 620, and that Edwin, Oswald and Oswiu were kings of Northumbria over the years 616-32, 633-41, 641-70—even though Oswiu's power was only accepted in Mercia from 654 to 657—we can see that over the period 560 to 657 it was normal for one or other of the leading kings to be regarded as *Bretwalda*. The series no doubt had gaps, but they were never long. It is clear that in the late sixth and seventh centuries, precisely at the time when the pattern of Angle and Saxon kingdoms was becoming established, and the mastery of the three giants, Northumbria, Mercia and Wessex, beginning to emerge, the idea was current that one great ruler could be lord over almost all Britain. He had inherited the position of earlier British kings, and hence he was called ruler of *Britain*. But the *Bret-*

waldas were masters not of Britain but of England, and in their succession we witness the first adumbration of English unity.

The Christian *Bretwaldas*, Ethelbert, Edwin, Oswald and Oswiu, are the central lay figures of Bede's *History*. Ethelbert, the first Christian king, is treated with considerable respect; but it is clear that St. Augustine had many anxious moments before the king was safely baptised. Ethelbert was king of Kent, and his kingdom had many links with Christian Francia; his wife was a Frankish, Christian princess, and in her train there was a Christian bishop. Ethelbert could not therefore ignore the Christian claims, but he seems to have felt the natural suspicion of a husband, liking to imagine himself the dominant partner, of his wife's private religion. Ethelbert at first kept Augustine on the Isle of Thanet, safely surrounded by water; then he went to inspect him— taking due care to sit always in the open air, since he thought Augustine's magic would be more potent indoors. To Augustine's preaching he gave a cautious reply, but established the Christian missionaries in Canterbury, and allowed them to work among his people. In due course Ethelbert was himself baptised, and gave the Church important patronage. But he was in no hurry—the delays made the Christian leaders very impatient—and refused to enforce Christianity on his followers. By the time of his baptism his power was waning, so that the Church under his aegis spread only, and temporarily, as far as London; and after his death even in Kent there was a pagan reaction.

Meanwhile Rædwald, the pagan king of East Anglia, had succeeded Ethelbert as *Bretwalda*. We know little about him; but the splendour of Sutton Hoo, once attributed to him, but now generally thought to belong to one of his successors a generation later, reflects the glory of his court; and he was responsible for setting the next *Bretwalda*, Edwin, on the throne of Northumbria. Bede tells the story of how Edwin as a young exile from his kingdom took refuge with Rædwald, and how Ethelfrith of Northumbria bribed Rædwald to have him killed. Edwin learned of the plan, and while he was sitting up late at night waiting for a friend to help him to escape, he had a vision of an unknown man (in the form, as it seems, of Paulinus) who told him that he would become a great king, the greatest the English people had known; and asked him if he would in return accept the faith of him who had given Edwin this promise of future greatness. Rædwald meanwhile had been admonished by his queen not to surrender their guest for gold, but rather to win back his kingdom for him. When the vision had disappeared, Edwin learned of Rædwald's change of mind; and soon after, at the battle of the Idle, Ethelfrith was defeated and killed, and Edwin made king of Northumbria. Some years later Paulinus came to preach the Christian faith to Edwin. At first the king did not recognise the man who had come to him in his dream; but presently Paulinus learned by divine revelation that a man in his likeness had given Edwin this prophecy. So he went to the king, laid his right hand on his head, and asked him if he recognised the sign. Edwin was terrified and immediately made preparations to fulfil his promise and accept the Christian faith. This was not, however, the only story told of Edwin's conversion.

Edwin is one of the most attractive characters in Bede's pages: a fine warrior, and a shrewd, kindly, honourable man. He was brought up a pagan. In due course he married Ethelbert's daughter; Ethelbert was dead, but the reigning king of Kent insisted that Edwin's queen be allowed to exercise her Christianity, and was reluctant to let her marry a pagan at all; to this Edwin replied that he would give due consideration to the Christian faith, and allowed the Christian Bishop Paulinus to preach to his people. Next year, on Easter night, King Edwin narrowly escaped death at the hands of an assassin; and the same night the queen gave birth to their first child, a daughter. The king, according to the story passed on by Bede, offered thanks to his gods; but Paulinus, at the same moment, began to offer thanks to Christ, and to assure the king that it was his prayers to Christ which had enabled the queen to have a safe and not too painful delivery.

The assassin was an emissary from the king of the " West

Saxons ", and Edwin had already planned an expedition of revenge. He promised Paulinus that, if he was successful, he would give up his own gods and become a Christian. He won a notable victory, and on his return to Northumbria gave up worshipping his idols. But he was still cautious about accepting Christianity. " He was by nature the shrewdest of men, and sat often alone in silence, discussing with himself in the depths of his heart what he should do, to which religion he should adhere."

The baptism of Edwin was a great event in Northumbrian history, and many stories were circulated about it. Bede tells three, all of which imply a period of hesitation; but it may be that the hesitation was increased by his attempt to fit all three tales into his narrative; and he has wholly omitted a fourth (if he knew it at all), by which not Paulinus but a leading Celtic churchman actually performed the rite of baptism. The story we have already told is a kind of tale common in the stories of royal conversion in the early Middle Ages; the king is forced to admit Christ's superior power. The second is also of a common type—the dream he had in youth which we have already described. The third is *sui generis*; the famous story of the debate in the royal council. " The life of men on earth," one of the leading warriors is reported as saying, " when compared to that which is beyond our knowledge, is as if you were sitting in your hall at dinner with your ealdormen and thegns in winter, with a fire in the midst and the hall aglow with warmth, but outside winter storms of rain or snow, and a sparrow flew very swiftly through the hall—in at one door, out at the other in a flash. While it is within, winter weather touches it not; but in a second its moment of peace is gone, and it is lost to your view. So the life of man is seen for a short while: what follows, what has gone before, we know not at all. If this new teaching has brought some firmer knowledge, it seems worth following." The debate ends with the high priest in person rushing off to deface his altars; and Edwin and all his people are baptised.

If Edwin was indeed baptised by a Celt (which is perhaps

unlikely), the cold truth is that these stories are mythical because two at least assume he was baptised by Paulinus; and one cannot help feeling that in Bede's pages, Edwin was converted not once but three times over. But whether any of them is precisely true matters little: the story of the sparrow was told in the eighth century if not in the seventh; it warms the cold earth of Yeavering in either case; and the sparrow is as secure of immortality as King Edwin. Furthermore, these stories show that Edwin was a character: a man about whom stories passed from hand to hand, who entered into legend. No other early English king had so good a press as Edwin; and to find a comparable group of stories one has to turn to Clovis, the maker of the Frankish kingdom, whose legendary image is vividly revealed to us in the first book of Gregory of Tours' *History of the Franks*. Clovis was a bloodthirsty ruffian who built up a great empire; and he did it, we are told, as much by fraud as by force. In Gregory's pages he wins kingdoms by practical jokes; he is for ever expressing naïve surprise that new territories, new opportunities for plunder, keep turning up—although he had been plotting hard for them. Clovis is an inverted Micawber. The personality revealed has only three points of contact with Edwin: each was a highly successful warrior king; each was (so the story goes) converted to Christianity because the Christian God won a victory for him; and because of his conversion, in the eyes of Gregory and Bede, each had God's support. Edwin is portrayed as the intellectual warrior; for ever hesitating, thinking up new tests. The portrait is as attractive as that of Clovis (however entertaining) is unattractive; and Bede rounds it off with a picture of the peace and prosperity of Edwin's later years. We cannot tell if the portrait is true; but we learn much of Bede's ideal of a great Christian king.

The golden age of Edwin's later years was shattered in 632, when an alliance between the pagan Penda of Mercia and the Christian Cadwallon, king of North Wales, defeated Edwin's army. Edwin himself was killed; Paulinus fled; his church collapsed. But Christianity was not entirely forgotten. At least one of the mission stayed on; a new Christian king

presently arose in Oswald, who was to become the martyr of
the Northumbrian church; and from the north and west the
influence of the Celtic missionaries was being increasingly
felt.

Oswald was a Christian from the start of his reign; he
built up the largest empire yet seen in England, and was
acknowledged overlord (so Bede tells us) by people talking all
the languages of Britain: Welsh, Pictish, Gaelic and English.
He restored the Northumbrian church by summoning a
bishop from Iona to Lindisfarne. Of the saintly Aidan Bede
paints one of his most celebrated clerical portraits; it is
wholly sympathetic, enthusiastic indeed, and wholly attractive. Aidan, in fact, would have been without blemish in
Bede's eyes but for one extraordinary failing. He celebrated
Easter on the wrong day.

Behind this dispute lay a long tradition: the Celtic
churches had had for many generations scant contact with the
churches of the Continent, and retained ancient customs (like
the method of deciding the date for Easter) and developed
customs of their own. These differences led to conflict when
the churches once more came into close contact. The conflict
was not one of doctrine; nor was there any formal schism.
The two churches met and mingled in various parts of Britain
in the seventh century, sometimes with more friction, sometimes with less. Aidan, the Celt, was always Oswald's
bishop; yet this did not detract from Oswald's sanctity in
Bede's eyes. Oswald died in battle, as Edwin had done; the
victim once again of an alliance formed by the Mercian
Penda. The place of his death became a centre of pilgrimage;
miracles were performed in his name. Oswald became the
saint and martyr, *par excellence*, of the Northumbrians; he
was the " most Christian king ".

Oswald was succeeded by his brother Oswiu, who in due
course revived his brother's power; and in 654 avenged his
predecessors by destroying Penda's last alliance in the battle
of *Winwæd*, where great numbers of English leaders were
killed. Some—perhaps including the king remembered at
Sutton Hoo—were swept away by the river, which was in

flood. For a short time Oswiu ruled Mercia; even after its independence had revived, he was the leading monarch in England until his death in 670. But his troubles were not over.

The powerful figure of St. Wilfrid had already appeared on the scene. He was then at the beginning of his long career, but already trained in Roman ways at Rome itself. Oswiu's wife, a daughter of King Edwin, had been brought up in Kent, and so was accustomed to the Roman Easter; and his son King Alchfrith was a pupil of St. Wilfrid. "Whence it sometimes is said to have happened in those days that Easter was celebrated twice in one year, and when the king had forgotten his fast and was celebrating Easter, the queen was still deep in Lent celebrating Palm Sunday." The Easter controversy may seem to us trivial, but its results were extremely conspicuous and awkward. It was not only the catering staff who would suffer in a household in which the queen fasted while the king caroused; small wonder that Oswiu determined to resolve the issue. Bede gives an elaborate account of the controversy between learned men on both sides. Rome and Wilfrid, and the queen, were victorious. The Synod of Whitby, in which the decision was taken, was a crucial step in the reabsorption of the Celtic churches into western Christendom. Both parties were the gainers; each had much to contribute to the other; and it is no coincidence that Northumbria, and England at large, in the generations following Whitby, in the age of Theodore and the age of Bede, saw a Christian civilisation with Roman and Celtic roots such as could hardly be paralleled on the Continent in this period.

CHAPTER VI

INTERLUDE: 670-871

After Oswiu's death no Northumbrian king ever stood so high, or was proclaimed *Bretwalda*. They were not nonentities; several make their bow in the pages of Bede, as fine warriors, as men of learning, even sometimes as monks; but none seemed to be of the stature of the three *Bretwaldas*, who had made Northumbria Christian, and helped to set a stamp on the English Church at large. The frontier of England and the Scottish kingdoms was not fixed for many centuries to come—save that it lay well to the north of its present line in the estimation of the rulers of Northumbria. The frontier with Wales was now coming into prominence: the frontier which was giving its name (so it seems) to Mercia, which was shortly to be the greatest of the English kingdoms. This reveals that the line was beginning to be stabilised. In the seventh century the march gave its name to an English kingdom; in the eighth the rulers of that kingdom gave definition to the march. The dykes of "Wat" (or Wade) and Offa are the most formidable monuments now surviving to any pre-conquest kings. Wat's dyke belongs to the mid-eighth century, in all probability, it seems, to the time of Ethelbald (716-57). The dyke, like the reign of Ethelbald, was a dress rehearsal for the work of Offa; without it Offa's achievement would hardly have been possible. But it is no chance that the author of the earlier dyke was soon forgotten, and that it was associated with the legendary Wade, an antique figure from the days of Teutonic paganism, while the dyke which followed it has always been Offa's dyke; and even though it by no means follows the present political boundary, it is in a deep sense the frontier of Wales. For a Welshman to live a few yards the wrong side of Offa's dyke is still a disgrace, even

99

though Offa's warriors no longer patrol it to keep the Welsh out of England.

If patrol it they ever did. The dykes are essentially boundaries, not defensive works. They made the frontier clear, made it easy to check that the Welsh tribes were not infiltrating; in some sectors they provided magnificent views into Wales; but they were not designed, like Hadrian's wall, for permanent observation. Even Offa could not hope to garrison an earthwork running the whole length of the Welsh frontier. Wat's dyke ran from the Dee estuary down into Shropshire; Offa's from the Dee estuary (a little to the west of Wat's) to the Bristol Channel. A part of the way it followed the line of the river Wye, so that nature provided the boundary. In a few other places, especially in the north, it was never completed. But it remains a magnificent achievement. In recent years it has been surveyed in detail by Sir Cyril Fox, and his results are laid out in his book *Offa's Dyke* (1955); with the aid of his text, his maps and plans and photographs it is possible to explore Offa's dyke and enjoy at the same time the fascination of observing the techniques of field archaeology at their most refined, and of seeing one of the great engineering achievements of the Dark Ages reconstructed. The concentration of effort, the vast labour force needed over so wide an area, reveals the energy and determination of Offa; the skilled alignment of the dyke, the use made of natural features, the improvement in technique over Wat's dyke, reveal the experience and skill of the engineer who designed it. Over the whole a single mind presided; but local differences in technique show that various sections were organised by local officials, as we should expect. Their failure in the north to complete the work allotted to them may be due to inefficiency in this sector, or to inadequate resources in a part of England in all probability very sparsely populated; or it may reveal that Offa was less anxious about this part of his frontier.

Offa bore an unusual name: technically, it is a shortened form of a longer name. Whether on his parents' initiative, or (as is quite possible) on his own, he was the one ruler of Mercia to bear the name of the great king of continental "Angel" from whom the Mercian kings claimed to be descended. Of the first Offa we know little; but in the mysterious ragbag of legendary references known as *Widsith*, we are told: "Offa ruled Angel, Alewih the Danes: he was the bravest of all these men, yet he did not perform mighty deeds beyond Offa; but Offa, first of men, while still a youth, gained the greatest of kingdoms; no one of the same age achieved greater deeds of valour in battle: with his single sword he fixed the boundary against the Myrgings at Fifeldor." We do not know if Offa knew *Widsith*, but we cannot doubt that he knew the legends of his great namesake; nor that they stirred him to fix the boundary against the Welsh.

It is perfectly clear that Ethelbald and Offa regarded themselves as successors of the earlier *Bretwaldas*, and with reason. But the little that we know of Ethelbald strongly suggests that he was by nature a ruthless barbarian. Towards the end of his career he drew on himself a stern rebuke from St. Boniface and other bishops of English birth working in Germany: his sins were having an evil effect on his people; the place for nuns was within their convents; the privileges of churches must be respected. Boniface acknowledged that Ethelbald kept the country at peace and was generous in almsgiving; but his rebuke and other hints prepare us for the dénouement: in 757 Ethelbald was murdered by his followers.

Offa, like Ethelbald, was strong and ruthless; also like Ethelbald, we know very little about him as a person. But what we do know reveals a width of interest and capacity which sets him quite apart from any of his predecessors. In his later years he was "king of the English", and this was no idle boast. We have no coherent narrative of his reign; but from the evidence of charters it has been possible to reconstruct in outline the stages by which he spread his power over the whole of the south of England, often, it is clear, against stiff local opposition, sometimes suffering reverses. But at the end of his life he was undisputed master of England south of the Humber, and Northumbria was in the hands of a respectful son-in-law. He was the only western monarch of the age treated as an equal by Charlemagne—the two great men cultivated each other's friendship, at least in a formal way. His reign saw the first substantial English silver currency, the effective start of the silver " penny ", which was to provide England with the basis of a money economy from the eighth to the fourteenth century, when a gold coinage was added to it. He took an interest in England's foreign trade. He was the patron of several monasteries, and showed his power by making Mercia the seat (for a brief time) of an archbishopric.

In 787 he had his son Ecgfrith anointed king of the Mercians to secure an orderly succession. But the plan miscarried. Ecgfrith survived his father only by a few months; the kingdom passed to a distant kinsman, and the Mercians never again wielded the authority of Offa. They were the leading power for another quarter of a century; but in 825 Egbert of Wessex defeated the Mercian king at the battle of *Ellendun,* and supremacy passed to Wessex. For a time Egbert was master of all the south of England, and so earned (at least in his subjects' eyes) the title *Bretwalda.* From 830 Mercia was independent once again; but Egbert continued to be overlord of the rest of southern England. The kingdom of East Anglia still had a native dynasty, commonly under West Saxon suzerainty, until 870, when it was finally destroyed by the Danes. Kent, Sussex, and Essex were kingships dependent on the West Saxon house; and were handed out from time to time by Egbert and his son and successor Æthelwulf as " kingdoms " for one or other of their sons. In effect, there were now three English kingdoms, Wessex, Mercia and Northumbria; and " England " was a concept not wholly unheard of.

The future lay with Wessex; and this was due, partly to the dynasty of Egbert, partly to the Danes. Already, in Egbert's time, the first serious Danish raid had occurred.

Through the middle of the century they grew fiercer and more frequent: in 865 a major invasion was staged; the Danes had come to settle. East Anglia, Northumbria and Mercia became their victims; only Wessex survived; and even Wessex it seems would not have outlived the 870s but for the heroic defence organised by Egbert's grandson Alfred.

CHAPTER VII

ALFRED

The accession of Alfred was a very singular event. In the first place, it was surprising that he should ever have become king at all. His father Æthelwulf is known to have had six children: Athelstan, Ethelbald, Ethelbert, Ethelred, Æthelswith (his one known daughter) and Alfred.[8] His eldest brother died before his father; the three others ruled Wessex in turn. When Ethelred died in 871, he left two sons; but both were minors, and only an experienced leader could hope to save Wessex from the Danes. Alfred's succession was undisputed, although one of his nephews tried to win the throne after his death.

In the second place it was singular that at the crucial moment Wessex should fall into the hands of the most inspiring king of his line; a man with the determination and imagination to plan a really successful defence, to leave his kingdom with some hope of future security. Even more surprising, Alfred found time to let his imagination roam in other fields; to think of monasteries and libraries and books which even laymen could read.

There is much about Alfred's life which would be wholly dark to us if we lacked Asser's biography. But it must be admitted that Asser often informs us only to tantalise: the curtain is lifted, only to be dropped again; Asser is devoted, wordy and clumsy.

It is clear that Alfred's life was even more difficult than we should expect. He was brought up to be pious and ignorant; he suffered constantly from fear of his own failings and shortcomings; and from physical disorders of a grotesque kind partly perhaps the result of mental anxiety. His career and writings were those of a man fundamentally healthy and

---

[8] The names were originally even more alliterative than they appear in the text, since all began with the diphthong Æ.

sane; but Asser's marvellously confused account of his ill-
nesses and anxieties shows that this sanity was won at a price.
The worst affliction struck him on his wedding day, and this,
Asser plainly implies, was no coincidence. We are given a
vision of a man of strong imagination, anxious and tempera-
mental; always afraid of himself, afraid of illness and incapacity to the point of hypochondria, aware of a larger world
than he himself lived in, desperately keen to live in it, and to
enable others to live in it.

Here is Asser's summary of his career. "Though established in royal power, the king was wounded by the nails of
many tribulations. From his twentieth to his forty-fifth year
(in which he now is) he has been troubled incessantly by the
severe visitation of an unknown disease; never an hour
passes but he either suffers from it, or is nearly desperate
from fear of it. He was troubled too (not without cause) by
the constant attacks of foreign peoples by land and sea which
he bears without intermission. What shall I say of his
numerous campaigns and battles against the heathen, of the
ceaseless problems of government? Of his daily concern for
the peoples who live from the Tyrrhenian Sea (the Adriatic)
to the far side of Ireland? We have seen and read letters and
gifts sent him from Jerusalem by the patriarch Elias. What
of the cities and towns he has restored and the new ones he
has built where none were before? What of the buildings in-
comparably adorned with gold and silver on his instructions?
What of the royal halls and chambers wonderfully built of
stone and wood at his command? What of the royal manor
houses of stone moved from their ancient sites and splendidly
built in more suitable places by royal edict? His illness apart,
his worst trouble was the obstructiveness of his own people,
who would not willingly submit to any, or very little, toil for
the common need of the kingdom. But he stood alone,
dependent on divine assistance; like a skilful helmsman
struggling to bring his vessel, loaded with much riches, to the
longed-for, safe harbour of his own land; though all his
sailors were nearly worn out, he did not permit the helm of
government, once he had taken it over, to quiver or turn,

though sailing amid the diverse raging whirlpools of this present life. He took every pains gently to teach, flatter, exhort, command, finally, after long patience, sharply to punish the disobedient, and to abhor in every way common foolishness and obstinacy; and so he wisely grasped and bound to his will and the common good of his whole kingdom his bishops, ealdormen and nobles, his dearest thegns, and also his reeves, to whom after God and the king the kingdom's power is seen to be subject, as is right. Sometimes through the people's laziness royal commands were not carried out; or tasks begun late were not finished and so of no use—I could mention fortifications ordered by him but not yet begun, or begun too late to be finished. Then the enemy's troops attacked by land or sea, or (as often) by both together; and the folk who had obstructed the royal commands were filled with shame and useless penitence."

As a boy Alfred twice visited Rome. In 853, at the age of four, his father sent him to stay at the court of Pope Leo IV, who robed him as a consul and treated him as his son. Two years later Alfred visited Rome again, this time in his father's company. King Æthelwulf was following in the footsteps of Cædwalla and Ine; but death did not come, and so, after lingering a twelvemonth, he returned home, to find his eldest surviving son in rebellion. The kingdom was divided between them, until the death of Æthelwulf two years later. Meanwhile Alfred had had a vision of Rome, ancient and modern, and had visited the Frankish court. But Latin literature was still a closed book to him; nor could he read and write. He was brought up, a favourite younger son, to love hunting, to love the Saxon poems he heard recited in his father's court; to dream, perhaps, of the kingdom to which he thought Pope Leo had anointed him; but with little prospect of achieving it. He grew up conscientious to a fault, but also imaginative and ambitious.

One of his gifts was an exceptional memory. His mother showed his brothers and himself one day a manuscript of Saxon poetry, and promised to give it to whichever learned it by heart the quickest. Alfred was stirred by the opportunity to outdo his elder brothers; also, Asser tells us, by the beauty of the initial letter on the first page. He took the book to his master, who read it to him; and he went back to his mother and recited what he had heard. Later he learned the daily office, and certain psalms and prayers, and had them written in a book which he always carried with him " as I have seen myself ". But he was still unable to read for himself. In later life he complained that there were no good scholars in Wessex. There was some truth in this; but it hardly excuses his failure to read and write. These were not accomplishments normal in royal children; but one cannot help feeling the mature Alfred excused the failings of his earlier years somewhat too readily. None the less he grew up with some understanding of Latin; able to follow the services of the church—to attend daily office, observe the day and night hours, hear daily mass with comprehension; and his piety was not conventional; he used also, in later life, to visit churches to pray—by night, so that his followers should not know that he did it.

We first hear of Alfred engaged in campaigning early in 868, when he was second-in-command to his brother King Ethelred against the Danes. He was then 18 (or 19), which seems to us an early age to command an army; but many medieval warriors were veterans by the time they reached 20, and we may be reasonably sure that this was not Alfred's first taste of warfare. In 868 the brothers were fighting in Mercia, in a vain attempt to save the Mercian kingdom from collapse. In 871 they were fighting in Wessex itself. In the same year Ethelred died, and Alfred was left in sole command. Year after year he fought inconclusive engagements with the Danes, gradually gaining experience but losing territory. In 878 the Danish army made a surprise attack in the middle of winter, when the West Saxon army was scattered about the country, on its manors and farms and small holdings.

" In this year the host went secretly in midwinter after Twelfth Night to Chippenham ", says the *Chronicle*, " and rode over Wessex and occupied it, and drove a great part of

the inhabitants oversea, and of the rest the greater part they
reduced to submission, except Alfred the king; and he with a
small company moved under difficulties through woods and
into inaccessible places in marshes. . . . And the Easter after,
King Alfred with a small company built a fortification at
Athelney, and from that fortification, with the men of that
part of Somerset nearest to it, he continued fighting against
the host. Then in the seventh week after Easter he rode to
Ecgbryhtesstan [Egbert's stone], to the east of Selwood, and
came to meet him there all the men of Somerset and Wiltshire and that part of Hampshire which was on this side of
the sea,[9] and they received him warmly. And one day later he
went from those camps to Iley Oak, and one day later to
Edington; and there he fought against the entire host, and
put it to flight, and pursued it up to the fortification, and laid
siege there a fortnight; and then the host gave him prelimin-
ary hostages and solemn oaths that they would leave his
kingdom, and promised him in addition that their king would
receive baptism."

To this Asser adds nothing of moment; but a twelfth-
century chronicle largely based on Asser, the *Chronicle of St.
Neot's*, has added to this famous story one yet more famous.
"As we read in the *Life* of the holy father Neot, Alfred long
lay hid in the home of a cowherd. It happened one day that
a peasant woman, the cowherd's wife, was preparing to cook
some loaves, and the king was sitting by the fire preparing
bow and arrows and other weapons. Presently the unfor-
tunate woman saw the loaves set by the fire burning; she
rushed up and removed them, upbraiding the most uncon-
quered king, and saying [in Latin hexameters]: ' You wretch,
you're only too fond of them when they're nicely done; why
can't you turn them when you see them burning?' The un-
fortunate woman had no idea that he was King Alfred, who

---

[9] This means either " those to the west of Southampton Water ",
and indicates that the author lived in the south-west of England, or
" those who were still in England " as opposed to those who had
fled overseas when the Danes invaded Wessex.

fought so many battles, won so many victories against the heathen."

We cannot tell whether the story has any basis of truth, but we can be sure it lost nothing in the telling. The earliest known version is a sermon about St. Neot, a Cornish saint, which was probably written in the eleventh or very early twelfth century. In this version the king is in no way at fault: he actually turns the loaves (or cakes). The better-known story given above is an embroidered version, written in the priory of St. Neots in Huntingdonshire later in the twelfth century. Clearly Alfred's memory was not held in respect there: in this later version St. Neot reproves the king in early life for tyrannical behaviour, and prophesies disaster; and the loaves are badly scorched.

Disaster was averted, and the six weeks on the isle of Athelney proved the turning point of Alfred's career. One would dearly like to know more of the secrets of King Alfred's underground movement; of the means by which he summoned the militia to Egbert's stone. About this we can only make guesses; but we can make something more than guesses about the reflections which this crisis stirred in Alfred's mind. It is clear that it revealed to him, in a new way, the weakness of Wessex in face of the Danish menace. The Danes were mobile; could attack both by land and by sea; they could achieve surprise, and overwhelm Wessex before the English militia could be summoned. The Danes formed the practice of fortifying a camp, or rather taking over an old fortification and using it as a base. In 878, while the Danes were operating in this way from Chippenham, Alfred took a leaf out of their book, and organised Athelney, hidden in the Somerset marshes, as a base for counter-attacks. The battle of Edington was decisive, not because it ended the Danish threat to Wessex—that was not lifted until after Alfred's death—but because it showed that it was possible for the Danish host to be heavily defeated, and because of the measures which Alfred took to follow up his victory.

His first action, to insist on the baptism of King Guthrum

and other leaders, seems to us both high-handed and utopian; it looks as if he thought that forcible baptism would civilise the barbarian. High-handed I think it was, an act of ruthless, conventional piety; but it also seems to show another side of King Alfred. Already he reckoned himself responsible for the well-being of English folk under Danish rule; and he clearly hoped by this step to save them from religious persecution by the pagan Danes.

In the years which followed Edington he set in motion a fundamental reorganisation of the defences of Wessex. The army consisted in the main of the king's followers or thegns and the peasant militia or fyrd. Each was divided, so that a part of the total force could serve as something approaching a standing army, ready under arms in case of attack; while the rest were tilling the soil or running their estates. Each part took their turn, so that the duty was fairly distributed. Next Alfred arranged for the fortresses of Wessex to be restored and occupied, and for new ones to be built. When this was finished, early in the next reign, a network of fortresses was spread all over southern England. They were large enclosures, surrounding areas some of which were already beginning to grow into towns. The word " borough " indeed is derived from the Old English *burh*, a fortress; and it was from the marriage of market places and walls to protect them that many English boroughs were formed. The two centuries after Alfred's death saw striking growth in English towns; and one of the reasons for this was the security which their walls gave to them, and the larger security which Alfred's fortresses gave to the country at large. Their immediate purpose was mainly military. When the Danes attacked, the folk of the neighbourhood could take shelter behind their walls; and their garrisons could use them as bases from which to attack the Danes. They formed a defence in depth, and for the first time made it possible for the defenders of Wessex to look forward to raids with some degree of confidence, and take rapid initiative against the raiders when they came (*figure 6b*).

The Danes were still, however, more mobile than the English; and Alfred's third plan was designed to meet them before they landed. He had large, speedy ships built, according to the *Chronicle*, to his own specification.

These measures did not abolish the Danish menace. Few of Alfred's later years were free from wars, none from rumours of wars. Shortly after 886 he made another truce with Guthrum, and settled the frontier between their kingdoms; but in the 890s another large Danish army battened on England and raided into Alfred's territory, and the Danes in the north were a permanent menace. None the less, it was possible for Wessex to breathe again; to imagine a future in which she would be secure; and this she owed to Alfred's imaginative plans of defence. They were widely admired at the time; and his *burhs* and his reorganisation of the militia were copied by the most powerful European monarch of the next generation, Henry the Fowler, the first Saxon king of Germany (919-36), in planning the defences of Saxony against the Magyars or Hungarians. But as one looks closely at Alfred's measures, and at all the striking innovations which have made him famous, one is struck not only by their novelty; but by how slow he was to devise them. He had been king nearly seven years when the crisis of 878 struck him, and a general longer than that. In this period he seems to have done nothing to improve the defences of Wessex; but to have been content with continuing the methods of his brothers, which had already proved at best indecisive, and at worst disastrous. Suddenly, on the verge of thirty, a new dimension was added to his mind. He was a man whose powers matured slowly, who became increasingly capable of absorbing new interests and learning from new experience.

This comes out most clearly in his intellectual pursuits. Alfred was brought up illiterate, though not wholly ignorant. As he grew to maturity, the ambition to have learned men about him grew too; and Asser likens him to a bee in his pursuit of scholars, flying away from home, alighting on diverse blossoms, taking what it fancies, and carrying it home. Alfred's store of honey contained four Mercians, including Werferth, bishop of Worcester (873-915), Plegmund, archbishop of Canterbury (890-914); one native of northern France, called Grimbald, and one continental Saxon, called John; and one Welshman, Asser himself. Their work developed slowly, and Alfred's efforts to revive monastic life, with John and Grimbald's help, achieved little. At a fairly early stage Alfred seems to have had the idea of making the riches of Christian literature available to more of his people by having them translated. But it was only slowly that he came to join in the work himself.

Asser tells us at length the story of how he came to join Alfred's seminar of learned men. There is something almost pathetic about the king's anxiety to have the company of this tedious, pedantic and naïve man; but Asser served him well. In the mid-880s, when Asser was first installed at the royal court, they used to sit together in the royal chamber, discussing subjects of common interest. One day Asser read to Alfred a passage which particularly struck him; and he produced the book of offices and prayers which he always carried with him, for Asser to copy the passage into it. But the book was full; so with the king's agreement, Asser prepared a new quire; and this was soon filled with passages chosen by the king.

When a passage had been written in the book, Alfred had the urge to read it, to turn it into English and pass it on to others. And so he determined to learn to read, and to read Latin; and in both these projects he took his first steps on the festival of St. Martin, 11 November 887, when he was 38 years old. It may be that Asser was a good teacher; it is even more likely that Asser was somewhat lumbering in his methods, and made Alfred impatient; no doubt the winter evenings gave him leisure for his lessons. How rapidly he advanced we cannot tell; he never dispensed with his seminar; we can never be entirely sure how much he did himself, how much he left to them; but between 892 and 899 five major works were translated into English, and of this operation Alfred himself was the director.

Alfred had visited Rome twice as a child; and had been devoted to the exercises of religion, at times neurotically devoted, at least from his teens. But his piety was conventional at root; and we cannot expect from a man who was illiterate till nearly 40 deep or original understanding of ancient texts. In taking to letters late in life he was following in the footsteps of Charlemagne; and we know that Asser was acquainted with Einhard's famous *Life of Charlemagne* and can assume that Alfred was too. Literacy enabled both of them to take a sympathetic interest in the work of the scholars of their court—much more than the external patronage affected by many medieval kings. Neither contributed anything original to the history of thought. But both have an honourable place in the history of learning and letters. Charlemagne personally inspired and directed a formidable revival of learning, and attempted to have his own sons and leading laymen as well as the clergy of his empire brought up to be literate and speak Latin. The intellectual revival cast long shadows before it and had many consequences; the palace school foundered after a brief life. Alfred worked on slighter foundations, with a less ambitious aim. He tried to spread the fruits of ancient wisdom by translating them into the vernacular. He directed the enterprise, as did Charlemagne; but imprinted his personality, not only on the enterprise, but also on the written word.

The books produced under Alfred's direction, or inspired by him, strongly suggest the lines of his interests. Early on Bishop Werferth translated Gregory the Great's *Dialogues* for him; and the next product of his seminar was Gregory's *Pastoral Care*. They enshrined for Alfred the wisdom of a great teacher: they taught by example—in the miracle stories of which the *Dialogues* are composed—and by precept, in the *Pastoral Care*, which laid emphasis on the bishop's duty to instruct, and to instruct laymen as well as clergy. In a special way, Alfred and Gregory had the same sources of inspiration; Gregory was one of the finest of the popes, a symbol of Roman greatness, and he was the pope who had sent Augustine to convert the English, the author of English

Christianity. Gregory was also one of the main characters of Bede's *History*, another of the works translated. The *Dialogues*, Bede and the universal history of Orosius (written in the early fifth century) all reflect an interest in the past; and in Alfred's time the traditions of his own people, and to a lesser extent of Rome and the Church at large, were collected in the *Anglo-Saxon Chronicle*, which he may have inspired, and almost certainly, like Asser, perused. But Alfred's interest in history was part of a wider interest in the world about him. To several of the translations he made his own characteristic additions. To the Orosius he added his own practical comments on the campaigns and political affairs of ancient history, and, above all, an original account of the geography of northern and central Europe, that part of Europe which had not been included in the Roman Empire. His searching curiosity was never more clearly revealed than in the way he tells the story of travellers who came to his court, and uses the information they could give him.

In his last two works he struck the personal note even more clearly. The Roman Boethius had written the *Consolations of Philosophy* while awaiting execution at the hands of the Goth Theodoric the Great. Alfred had lived to see his own world shattered by the Danes, and lived in constant expectation of disaster. Not infrequently he draws his readers from the heights of Roman philosophy to the concrete world in which they were living; and though there is a certain naïvety in his procedure, these asides are of great interest, and few men could have treated texts so cavalierly and got away with it. A passage from the Boethius illustrates his interests and his outlook to perfection. The words in italics bear some relation to what Boethius wrote; the rest are Alfred's own, though suggested apparently in part by an earlier commentary.

"*You know that covetousness and greed for worldly dominion never pleased me over much, and that I did not all too greatly desire this earthly rule*, but yet I desired tools and material for the work that I was charged to perform, namely that I might worthily and fittingly steer and rule the dominion that was entrusted to me. You know that no man can reveal any talent or rule and steer any dominion without tools and material. That without which one cannot carry on that craft is the material of every craft. This, then, is a king's material and his tools for ruling with, that he have his land fully manned. He must have men who pray, and soldiers and workmen. Lo, you know that without these tools no king can reveal his skill. Also, this is his material, which he must have for those tools—sustenance for those three orders; and their sustenance consists in land to live on, and gifts, and weapons, and food, and ale, and clothes, and whatever else those three orders require. And without these things he cannot hold those tools, nor without these tools do any of the things that he is charged to do. *For that reason I desired material to rule that dominion with, that my powers and dominion would not be forgotten and concealed.* For every talent and every dominion is soon worn out and silently passed over, if it is without wisdom; because no man can bring forth any craft without wisdom, for whatever is done in folly can never be accounted as a craft. In brief, I desired to live worthily as long as I lived, and leave after my life, to the men who should come after, my memory in good works."

In the last of the translations, Alfred's version of the first book of St. Augustine's *Soliloquies*, his thoughts turn from the uncertainties of the present life to the hope of future peace; the main theme is immortality. In the preface he explained his attitude to ancient learning, in the famous metaphor of the wood, from which he gathered " staves and props and bars . . . and crossbars and beams " and carried them home and built himself a house. " It is not to be marvelled at that one expends labour on such material both in the carriage and in the building; but every man, when he has built a village on land leased to him by his lord, with his help, likes to stay in it sometimes, and to go hunting and fowling and fishing, and to support himself in every way on that leased land, both on sea and land, until the time when through his lord's mercy he may acquire bookland and a perpetual inheritance. So shall the rich giver act, who rules both these transitory habitations and the eternal mansions.

May He who created both, and rules both, grant me that it may be in my power both to be useful here and to attain thither."

The purpose of his translations was to give others a chance to enjoy the wonderful products of his wood; and his methods can be seen in other of his activities. In his laws he started from the characteristic assumption that English law was somehow closely linked with divine law. The sources range from the Book of Exodus to the laws of his predecessors, kings of Wessex, Mercia and Kent; they are gathered together, and a selection made, freely made at the king's own choice, and then promulgated with the consent of the Witan.

Alfred was only 50 when he died; yet he had altered and developed rapidly in his later years; and his last books read like the reflections of an old man. He had certainly travelled a long way. The shrewd, mature, sophisticated simplicity of the *Soliloquies* is a far cry from the sensitive, neurotic enthusiasm of the boy who had learned Saxon poems by heart. His career shows how far a man could travel on the road to civilisation in a single lifetime; and how difficult it was to go thus far, even for a man with the talents and opportunities of Alfred. So wide was the range of his achievements, so attractive is the voice which speaks from his writings, so rare is it to be able to listen to the voice of a medieval king, that we are in danger of idealising him. He was after all human; in some respects, intensely human. But in a world falling into ruins he had the courage to plan for a happier future; not only to plan defence, but to plan for a fuller and richer life for his subjects. In this there is something heroic. The achievement is impressive; the vision astonishing.

CHAPTER VIII

THE TENTH CENTURY

Many of Alfred's talents were distributed among his descendants, who ruled Wessex and England from 899 to 1016. None achieved quite his width of interest. None was an author in his own right, and none had an Asser to tell us of his private life. They are shadowy figures compared with their distinguished forebear; but they were clearly not shadowy figures in their own day. Edward and Athelstan were distinguished soldiers, who greatly extended the area of Alfred's kingdom. From a purely military point of view the formation of the English kingdom owes as much to Edward as to Alfred; and no Saxon king save perhaps Offa was so widely known and respected in western Christendom as Athelstan. Edgar's reign was peaceful, but his grip on the country was as tight as, perhaps tighter than Athelstan's; and he was patron to a monastic and intellectual revival such as Alfred and Athelstan had dreamed of, but could not live to see. These were outstanding men; and although the kingdom decayed under Ethelred II, the Unready, its achievements had been very notable. But it is not easy to get any real glimpse of these kings as persons. If we wish to do so, we must concentrate on Athelstan and Edgar.

Edward the Elder had succeeded Alfred as king of Wessex. With the aid of his sister Æthelflæd, Lady of the Mercians, he set about the reconquest of the midlands and the southeast. When he died he was effective ruler of all England south of Trent; but the Mercian folk remembered that he was a West Saxon. He was succeeded by his son Athelstan, the natural heir of the West Saxon line, who had been brought up in Mercia, and so commanded the allegiance of the Mercians in a way which had been denied his father. Athelstan, indeed, was acknowledged king by the Mercians before he was acknowledged by the West Saxons.

Athelstan won recognition of his kingship over northern England and southern Scotland. He was king, *basileus*, even perhaps emperor of Britain. He substantially enhanced the notion of English kingship.

The centre of Athelstan's life was in his court, in his hall, where his warriors gathered round him and he dispensed gifts. When the *Chronicle* suddenly breaks into heroic verse, in the famous piece on the battle of *Brunanburh*, it calls the king " lord of warriors, ring-giver of men ". He was the heir of Hrothgar and Beowulf; but he was much more than that. The clerks who wrote his charters tried to impose upon the long-suffering Latin tongue their sense of his majesty by inflating the language in which they couched his solemn grants with strange outlandish words, often remotely derived from Greek, and portentous obscurity. On 28 May 934 one of these clerks inscribed a document granting an estate in Kent to a thegn. It is a masterpiece of hideous absurdity; and warns anyone who infringes it that he will burn with Judas the committer of impious treachery, a sentiment which does not suggest complete confidence in the effectiveness of human punishment. But in fact Athelstan's power was growing steadily more effective and more confident; and the list of the Witan gathered at Winchester who attached their crosses to this document is very impressive. On 7 June the same scribe wrote another charter, in similar terms, but of more ambitious purpose: the grant of Amounderness in Lancashire to the Archbishop of York—a grant whose authenticity has often been questioned, especially in Lancashire, but has in recent years been successfully defended. Almost exactly the same impressive list of signatories put their crosses to this instrument. They start with Athelstan himself, who in the body of the document calls himself " king of the English, elevated by the right hand of the Almighty, which is Christ, to the throne of the whole kingdom of Britain "; it continues with two archbishops, three sub-kings—Welsh princes—sixteen bishops, seven ealdormen, six Viking earls, eleven king's thegns, and thirteen other folk. The court was now at Nottingham, and the *Chronicle* explains rather tersely why this large gathering was moving rapidly north from Winchester: "In this year King Athelstan invaded Scotland both with a land and a naval force, and harried much of the country". The leading Welsh princes were already in his train; he now set to work to subdue the Scots. In this, however, he was not immediately successful. Three years later an Irish-Norse leader, in alliance with the kings of Scotland and Strathclyde, staged a major invasion of England itself. At a place called *Brunanburh*, whose situation we do not know, they were met by Athelstan and Edmund his brother; Athelstan's great victory is recorded in the stirring verse of a contemporary poet. No doubt the *Battle of Brunanburh* was recited before Athelstan in his equivalent of Heorot. On his way north he stopped at Chester-le-Street, where St. Cuthbert's relics lay, and his cathedral, later to be moved to Durham. To St. Cuthbert he presented a copy of Bede's *Lives* of the saint, made, perhaps, at Glastonbury, and at the beginning is a picture of the king presenting the book to the saint (*figure 6a*). Then he passed on to subdue Scotland; and for the remaining two years of his life his prestige was unquestioned, his power unchallenged.

Athelstan was the Pierpont Morgan of his age. As the clergy of Chester-le-Street saw the great army pass on into Scotland, and turned to enjoy their new acquisition, they may well have wondered whether the king would be remembered in future ages mainly as a great conqueror or as a princely collector. Like Pierpont Morgan, Athelstan collected books and works of art. Unlike the American millionaire, he also collected relics of saints, and was himself a connoisseur of all that he collected. He was a great giver of gifts; but the gifts in Athelstan's Heorot were more varied than in Hrothgar's; and so were the men who received them. Gold and silver ornaments, land, weapons, pieces of craftsmanship of every kind flowed through his hands; and also rare and beautiful books, interesting for their content as well as their appearance; and, above all, relics. He received gifts from all over Europe, gave richly in return, and gave especially to his followers, to his bishops and to churches in his own land. To

Canterbury cathedral he gave a Gospel Book which had belonged to the coarb (or abbot) of Armagh; and another Gospel Book which Athelstan had received from his brother-in-law, Otto the Great of Germany, on Otto's accession to the throne in 936. It is now in the Cotton collection in the British Museum, and it carries an inscription which opens with these words: " This volume of the gospels Athelstan emperor of the English and ruler of the whole of Britain (*Anglorum basyleos et curagulus totius Bryttannie*) with devout mind granted to the cathedral church dedicated to Christ, the first in the land, at Canterbury."

Otto the Great was the most eminent of Athelstan's continental friends; but he was one among many. William of Malmesbury, writing in the twelfth century, but using a much earlier Latin poem, lists a number of these: Harold, king of Norway, who sent an embassy to Athelstan at York, including among his gifts a ship with " a gold beak and purple sail, surrounded inside with a dense rank of gilded shields "; Henry I of Germany, who asked for Athelstan's sister as wife to his son Otto; Hugh the Great, duke of the Franks, and Conrad duke of Burgundy, who married two other sisters of the king. To these we could add the Carolingian Louis, later king of the Franks, called Louis d'Outremer because he was brought up in Athelstan's court. When Duke Hugh sent his request for an English princess, he chose his embassy and his gifts with canny skill. The leader of the party was Baldwin count of Flanders, whose wife was Athelstan's aunt; and " when he had set forth the wooer's requests in an assembly of nobles at Abingdon, he offered indeed most ample gifts, which might instantly satisfy the cupidity of the most avaricious: perfumes such as never before had been seen in England; jewellery, especially of emeralds, in whose greenness the reflected sun lit up the eyes of the bystanders with a pleasing light; many fleet horses, with trappings, ' champing ', as Maro [Virgil] says, ' on bits of ruddy gold '; a vase of onyx, carved with such subtle engravers' art that the cornfields seemed really to wave, the vines really to bud, the forms of the men really to move, and so clear and polished that it reflected like a mirror the faces of the onlookers; the sword of Constantine the Great, on which could be read the name of the ancient owner in letters of gold; on the pommel also above thick plates of gold you could see an iron nail fixed, one of the four which the Jewish faction prepared for the crucifixion of Our Lord's body; the spear of Charles the Great, which, whenever that most invincible emperor, leading an army against the Saracens, hurled it against the enemy, never let him depart without the victory; it was said to be the same which, driven by the hand of the centurion into Our Lord's side, opened by the gash of that precious wound Paradise for wretched mortals; the standard of Maurice, the most blessed martyr and prince of the Theban legion, by which the same king was wont in the Spanish war to break asunder the battalions of the enemies, however fierce and dense, and to force them to flight; a diadem, precious certainly for its quantity of gold, but more for its gems, whose splendour so threw flashes of light on the onlookers that the more anyone strove to fix his gaze on it, the more was he driven back and forced to give in; a piece of the holy and adorable Cross enclosed in crystal, where the eye, penetrating the substance of the stone, could discern what was the colour of the wood and what the quantity; a portion also of the crown of thorns, similarly enclosed, which the madness of the soldiers placed on Christ's sacred head in mockery of his kingship."

The gems sparkled; the king was delighted; his sister was shipped off with " hardly inferior presents ". The chronicler sees in his mind's eye the glory of the gifts; and for this he had a special reason. His own monastery, Malmesbury Abbey, was enriched with part of the Cross and Crown of Thorns " by the support of which, I believe, the place still flourishes " in spite of all the storms it has been through.

So much of the Middle Ages is gathered in this extraordinary accumulation of genuine works of art and bogus relics, that it is worth dwelling for a moment on it. How did it come about that Athelstan, and the monks of Malmesbury, thought so much of pieces of wood and bone, of antique and decrepit weapons; valued them both as earthly treasure with an earthly price, and heavenly treasure beyond payment? The logic is quite simple. The saints are in Heaven; but they care for men as much as ever, and where there is a fragment of their earthly body, there they will agree to have an earthly habitation; they will even see to it that God performs miracles there. By how much the more will not Christ himself perform miracles for those who have relics of his earthly life? They cannot have pieces of his earthly body, which rose from the Dead and ascended into Heaven, but Cross and Crown of Thorns and lance and garments were divided and redivided and spread over the world, and a new kind of celestial currency formed from relics of Christ and his saints. Granted the premise, the logic is clear enough; and the basic doctrine, of course, is still held among Roman Catholics to-day. But the chain has a weak link. It assumes that we can be sure that the relics are genuine. No one now doubts that the majority of medieval relics were spurious; they were not what they claimed to be; and for this reason the cult has fallen into general disrepute. It is fortunate that no one ever tried to reassemble the Cross or the Crown of Thorns or the garments of the Blessed Virgin. It has been estimated that the fragments of the " True Cross " circulating in the Middle Ages would have built a battleship; the Crown of Thorns would have hedged many acres; and no doubt St. Mary's wardrobe would have cast doubts on the notion that Our Lord came of poor family.

The story is told of an eminent painter who was shown what purported to be one of his own paintings by a friend. He knew perfectly well that it was not his; but to save his friend's feelings he immediately signed it. Innumerable saints were honoured by having bones of other people, and sometimes of animals, encrusted in silver and gold and gems, enclosed in altars, carried in processions, in their name. Perhaps they honoured the intention; allowed faith to conquer fiction; perhaps the weak link in the chain was by-passed. When St. Teilo died, so we are told by his biographer, three communities fought for his body; their troubles were resolved by the saint obligingly providing three bodies of himself. The saint died in the seventh century; the story was told in the twelfth. To us it is an example of how medieval logic could be applied to explain the inexplicable—since three bodies were known to exist; to most of its readers it must have seemed a happy example of celestial diplomacy and tact.

Athelstan's elder contemporary, Henry I of Germany, is supposed to have been as hard-bitten a ruler as one could find in Europe in his age. But late in life he bartered a large slice of territory—a portion of modern Switzerland—for another holy lance, a particularly potent talisman of victory, and an object supposed, like Athelstan's sword, to have belonged to Constantine, and to be a necessary possession for anyone aspiring to be Roman Emperor. Henry died soon after; but with the lance Otto his son conquered the Magyar hordes on the Lechfeld in 955, and with it he rode to Rome to be crowned emperor in 962.

Faith in the potency of relics was universal. What marked Athelstan out was the scale of his collection and the refinement of its contents. He was not a miser: he gave away much of what he collected; but he never ceased to gather, from all over Europe, what he could find, what his agents could buy. The church of Dol in Brittany wished to thank him for a favour, and wrote a letter to him. They promised to pray for him, and the prior wrote: " I send you relics, which we know you value more than earthly treasure—bones of St. Senator, and of St. Paternus and his master St. Scabillion, who died on the same day as he. These two lay right and left of St. Paternus: their solemnities like his are on 23 September." Athelstan was well acquainted with some of the churches of Devon and Cornwall, and had good relations with Wales, so he may well have known about some of the Celtic saints. The prior evidently assumes that he knows about Paternus; but that Senator and Scabillion will be new additions to Athelstan's collection. The relics of Paternus went to Malmesbury; his companions to the new church at Milton Abbas, founded by Athelstan himself, along with the letter to authenticate them; and there the letter was found 150 years or more later. Also to Milton went another fragment of Athelstan's part of the Cross, an arm and bones and the crozier of St. Samson, bishop of Dol, an arm of St. Branwalader, other relics sealed in five boxes " still closed "—which he had brought from Rome and from Brittany.

No inventory has survived of the relics which passed through Athelstan's hands, and any attempt to reconstruct a catalogue faces two serious difficulties. For the bulk of the collection we have no list at all; for a substantial part of it we have a list, but pious fraud has so enlarged it that we cannot tell what it originally contained. A century later Exeter Cathedral claimed to have a third of all the relics that King Athelstan brought from abroad. Westminster and Glastonbury Abbeys and other churches also claimed very substantial gifts, which have probably been inflated in the course of time. In handling relics special rules of morality applied. Lying may be sinful, but a lie about relics was very white, for those who benefited. Theft, however, was neither good nor bad; it was only possible if the saint himself wished to be moved, and the thief was thus merely the passive instrument of the saint's intentions. Kleptomania, to which avid collectors are often liable, could be regarded as pious zeal. When St. Hugh of Lincoln took a piece off their best relic with his teeth, the monks of Fécamp Abbey in Normandy were furiously indignant, but his biographer tells the story without a blush. The monks of Abingdon read the story of Duke Hugh's embassy to Athelstan, read the list of relics, and their mouths watered. Then they noted that the court took place at Abingdon. So pious a king could not possibly have stayed there without giving a notable present to the abbey. It was clear indeed, that he had given them a part of the Crown of Thorns, part of one of the nails, St. Maurice's standard and a finger of St. Denis, all in a silver chest. " Of this ", wrote Dr. Armitage Robinson, " we need only remark that it was a bold claim."

In 939 Athelstan died, still in the prime of life, at the height of his power. By extending his sway over Wales and Scotland and by his relations with the rulers of western Europe, he had added a dimension to the royal power of his predecessors. His princely accumulation of relics, however much it owed to the crank and the charlatan, added an extra dimension to the treasures of ancient Heorot. Like Alfred, he was literate, and he was evidently a man of considerable artistic taste; it is no coincidence that he was a patron of his relative, the artistic St. Dunstan. But we read about him through the haze of the foggiest court-Latin any country or any age produced; and as we pause for breath amid the interminable, grotesque periods of his charters, we cannot help feeling that he was something of a parvenu emperor. They remind us of the famous gloss in a preacher's sermon notes: "argument weak, shout like mad", and it has been suggested that they protest so much simply because he could not be sure of obedience. This, in Athelstan's case, may not be the whole truth; clearly he loved baroque splendour of every kind. But the protestation serves to remind us that only his prestige and success as a warrior kept the Vikings at bay; that the time was not far off when they would strike again.

Athelstan was succeeded by his brother Edmund, and he by his brother Eadred; both were conscientious monarchs about whom comparatively little is known; neither lived long. Then the kingdom passed, in quick succession, to Edmund's two sons, Eadwig and Edgar. Edgar was the last great king of Alfred's line; and, as Edgar started his career in rebellion against his elder brother, Eadwig has had a bad press. He quarrelled with St. Dunstan. We are told that the reason for the quarrel was that Eadwig left the banquet on his coronation day to engage in idle conversation with two ladies of doubtful virtue; that Dunstan was one of those who reproved him, and that he took it ill. Subsequently his misgovernment brought its due reward; Edgar was proclaimed king of Mercia in 957, and in 959 the dissolute Eadwig died. But Eadwig may only have been 13 when he was crowned, and is unlikely to have been much older; and he was probably under 20, perhaps well under 20, when he died. It is difficult to take any of this very seriously; and it is perfectly clear that Edgar also sowed his wild oats.

Edgar died in 975, aged 32. By then his childhood was long forgotten, and he had achieved enough to leave an indelible mark on English kingship. He was a friend of leading churchmen, and no doubt they saw to it that he received a good write-up; but it is clear that his achievement, for his age, was substantial. It is also clear that he owed much to his eminent clerical advisers, Dunstan of Canterbury, Oswald of York and Ethelwold of Winchester; how much, it is hard to say. He ruled England with a strong hand; he was known as Edgar the Peaceful, but his peace was a sign of strength not of weakness. He pushed the union of Danes and English a stage further; like Athelstan, his power was acknowledged by the other kings of the island. In 973 he was anointed and crowned with great solemnity; in the same year seven Welsh and Scottish kings submitted to him at Chester—though whether they really rowed him on the river Dee, as legend has it, we cannot tell. He was the patron of a great monastic revival.

Not unnaturally, the last item was the best recorded. The revival of monastic life, and with it of many types of learning, of art and architecture, is one of the most exciting events of the tenth century. Alfred and Athelstan had had comparatively little success in their attempts to patronise such a movement. Under Athelstan's immediate successors, the triumvirate of saints began their work. Under Edgar it came to fruition. What is of special interest to us is that they attributed their success to him. It shows how lofty a sense men had of the royal office that they should do this. The language they used has a familiar ring to-day, when we are used to hear dictators adulated as authors of all good things, including scientific discoveries. But there is this difference. It is doubtful if Edgar could read Latin; and it is doubtful therefore whether his courtiers needed to flatter him to this extent in the text of their treatise on monastic customs. This treatise, the *Regularis Concordia*, the *Monastic Agreement*, was probably written by St. Ethelwold; it clearly reflects both his views and Dunstan's. By invoking royal authority it attempts to weaken the grip of secular lords on monastic property and to plaster over cracks of disagreement between the monasteries. But it is perfectly clear that its author really believed, as did most churchmen in northern Europe in the tenth century, that the king was Christ's vicar on earth, chief repository of divine authority, mediator of divine blessings—not of the Eucharist, for a king was not a priest—but mediator of the scarcely less efficacious blessing of divine order and good government.

"Edgar the glorious, by the grace of Christ illustrious king of the English and of the other peoples dwelling within the bounds of the island of Britain, from his earliest years began to fear, love and worship God with all his heart. For while he engaged in the various pursuits that befit boyhood, he was nevertheless touched by the divine regard, being diligently admonished by a certain abbot who explained to him the royal way of the Catholic faith. Wherefore, lest the spark of faith, which was beginning gradually to brighten, should be extinguished by sloth and idleness, he began carefully and earnestly to consider by what holy and deserving works it could be made to burn with the brilliance and ardour of perfection." The preface goes on to describe, and exaggerate, the low state of monasticism at his accession, his labours and his wife's for its revival.

"When therefore the Rule of the holy father Benedict had been accepted with the greatest goodwill, very many of the abbots and abbesses with their communities of monks and nuns vied with one another in following in the footsteps of the saints; for they were united in one faith, though not in one manner of monastic usage. Exceedingly delighted with such great zeal the aforesaid king, after deep and careful study of the matter, commanded a Synodal Council to be held at Winchester. To this assembly he most humbly sent a letter, set forth magnificently on parchment and couched in encouraging and peaceable terms, in which, moved by the grace of Christ, he urged all to be of one mind as regards monastic usage, to follow the holy and approved fathers and so, with their minds anchored firmly on the ordinances of the Rule, to avoid all dissension, lest differing ways of observing the customs of one Rule and one country should bring their holy conversation into disrepute. Deeply moved by the wise advice of this excellent king, the bishops, abbots and abbesses were not slow in raising their hands to heaven in hearty thanksgiving to the throne above for that they were thought worthy to have so good and so great a teacher."

To a modern reader this adulation of Edgar is not attractive. But it seems likely that this strong, capable, wilful young man was in many ways an attractive person; at any rate his piety was genuine, for Ethelwold and his associates would not have written like this if it had been wholly absurd. This ideal of the religious king was to appear later in the German kingdom, in Henry II and Henry III; and the emperor Henry III, in 1046, carried it to the length of disposing of three popes, who were trying to occupy the Holy See at the same time, and instituting reform at the heart of western Christendom. From this reform in due course arose the doctrine—not a new one, but one very commonly ignored in the centuries immediately preceding—that it was for pope and bishops to regulate the Church not for kings; and out of the powerful doctrines of the papal reformers came the conflicts which we commonly call the investiture disputes. This lay far in the future in 970, when the *Concordia* was probably published. But already there were not wanting folk who observed that too close a lien of king and Church was not altogether healthy for the Church; that if the king was able to treat bishoprics and monasteries as pieces of personal property, he might use them for unsuitable ends. In Edgar's integrity Dunstan and Ethelwold trusted, and Edgar was not yet 30. But five years later, in 975, he suddenly died, and his young sons, and the factions who supported them, squabbled for his kingdom.

The party of Edward (who was about 13) argued that he was the elder and better candidate, and should be king. The party of Ethelred (who may not have been more than 6 or 7) had serious doubts about Edward's character. It was alleged much later that they also argued that Ethelred was born

1a   A Viking ship, reconstructed. *From the Oslo Museum*

1b   Ornamental purse-lid. *From Sutton Hoo Ship Burial, British Museum*

2 Offa's dyke on Llanvair Hill, Shropshire. *From a photograph by Dr. J. K. S. St. Joseph*

3*a, b, c* "Standard", helmet and whetstone. *From the Sutton Hoo Ship Burial, British Museum* (See page 203)

3*d* A Saxon cathedral: North Elmham, Norfolk. *From a photograph by Dr. J. K. S. St. Joseph*

4a   A passage from Beowulf. *From the British Museum, Cotton MS. Vitellius A.xv, f. 130v (c. 1000)*

4b   Domesday Book: a passage from the first page of Wiltshire enlarged (vol.1,f.64v). *Crown copyright, reproduced by permission of the Controller of H.M. Stationery Office a* The King in majesty, with orb and sceptre: coin of Edward the Confessor. *From the Ashmolean Museum*

b Edward the Confessor: forged seal. *From the British Museum*

c William II: genuine seal, reverse. *From the British Museum*

6a King Athelstan presents a book to St. Cuthbert. *From Corpus Christi College, Cambridge, MS. 183, f.1v.*

6b A Saxon fortified town: Wallingford, Berkshire. *From a photograph by Dr. J. K. S. St. Joseph (Crown Copyright reserved)*

7a   King Cnut and Queen Emma (Ælfgyfu) present a gift to the New Minster, Winchester. *From the British Museum, Stowe MS. 944.f.6*

7b   On his return from Normandy, Harold visits Edward the Confessor. *From the Bayeux Tapestry*

8a, e Gold rings of Æthelswyth, queen of Mercia (855–88) and
Æthelwulf, king of Wessex (839–58). *From the British Museum*

8b, c, d The Alfred Jewel. *From the Ashmolean Museum*

9 Anglo–Saxon Coins (*from the Ashmolean Museum*): *a* Ethelred
the Unready, *b* Cnut, with a helmet, *c* Edward the Confessor, *c.*
1053–6, *d* Edward the Confessor, 1065–6, *e* Harold II, 1066

9*f* The death of Edward the Confessor. *From the Bayeux Tapestry*

10a The coronation of Harold. *From the Bayeux Tapestry*

10b The death of Harold. *From the Bayeux Tapestry*

LLVM:AT HESTENGA CEASTRA

The Norman camp at
Hastings is fortified. *From
the Bayeux Tapestry*

The "White Tower",
keep of the Tower of
London. *Crown Copyright,
reproduced by permission of
the Ministry of Public
Building and Works*

12 The four Norman kings, by Matthew Paris, *c.* 1250. *From the British Museum, Royal. MS. 14.C.vii, f.8v.*

when his father was king and his mother queen; was *porphyrogenitus*, "born in the purple". It is very doubtful if they really argued so at the time, though not wholly impossible in a Europe still dominated by Otto the Great, whose succession to the throne of Germany had been challenged by his younger brother, on account of such a claim. But it is more likely that this suggestion belongs to the world of Henry I's early manhood, not the childhood of Ethelred.[10]

Whatever their grounds, the followers of Ethelred were not content to let Edward rule. On 18 March 978 Edward came to visit his brother at Corfe (Dorset). As he approached the hall where his brother was living, Ethelred's retainers came out and gathered round the king's horse, as if to greet him. But they greeted him with blows, stabbed him, and buried his body in Wareham, near by, with maimed rites or no rites at all; and the English people learned that violence and treachery had made Ethelred their king.

Edward was dead, but his career was by no means over. A year later the ealdorman of Mercia unearthed his remains, and had them solemnly translated to Shaftesbury. The story was told that they were marvellously uncorrupted; a whisper of miracles began to gather round the tomb. The young man's bones became holy relics; his brother was compelled to acknowledge him a saint, and to pronounce the day of his death a solemn festival. Thus was made King Edward the Martyr. When the ealdorman translated the body to Shaftesbury, he seems to have been performing an act of reconciliation; by doing honour to the murdered king, he seems to have hoped to rally Edward's supporters to Ethelred. If this explanation (hinted at by one contemporary) is correct, one may doubt if he was successful. The growing cult of Edward must have been a constant reminder to Ethelred of the manner of his accession. The murder was performed by Ethelred's retainers, so he could not escape some measure of responsibility. Since he may not have been more than 9 or 10 at the time, we find it difficult to take this charge very

[10] See pp. 25, 176-8.

seriously. But it cast a gloom over Ethelred's accession, and in a measure over his whole reign. The rapid growth of Edward's cult is very likely in part a reflection of growing political unrest. Ethelred failed to win or hold the allegiance of several of his leading thegns. The ealdorman of Mercia died in 983; in 985 his son and successor Ælfric was sent into exile, presumably for rebellion; in 992 one of the other leading ealdormen of Ethelred's early years, Ælfric of Hampshire, turned traitor; in 993 Ethelred tried to check his activities by blinding his son; yet ten years later Ælfric was in a position to turn traitor again. This illustrates the way in which some of Ethelred's leading supporters sat lightly to their allegiance, and one cannot help suspecting that the cult of Ethelred's dead brother was deliberately fostered by them; that Edward's bones became a rallying point for disloyalty and opposition; that the elder brother in his grave gave no peace to the younger brother on the throne. In Ethelred's code of 1008 it is specially noted that " the councillors decreed that Edward's festival is to be celebrated all over England on 18 March ", as if they wrung this decree from a reluctant king.

Dissidence and half-suppressed revolt had never been uncommon in Anglo-Saxon England. In Ethelred's time they walked openly. A thirteenth-century chronicler records that he was known as Ethelred *Un-ræd*; from which the modern corruption " the Unready " is derived. The chronicler is late,[11] but he had access to information now lost, and the pun is so clever that it seems not at all unlikely that it was given to Ethelred by a contemporary wit. " Ethelred " is a compound of two Old English words, *æthel* and *ræd*, meaning noble counsel. *Unræd* meant " no counsel ". But it had overtones and alternative meanings; and these included " evil counsel " and " a treacherous plot ". Ethelred was king, according to his charters, " by the grace of God ", or, more precisely, " with the divine approval pre-ordained by the grace of the same our God and Lord ". This may have com-

---

[11] But the nickname was almost certainly known to Walter Map, writing in the late twelfth century (*De Nugis Curialium*, trans. M. R. James, 1923, p. 228 and n.).

forted him; but he was never allowed to forget that there were other words which could be used to describe the manner of his accession. His brother's murder blighted his career; he could never escape the curse of Cain.

"Unræd" could imply that Ethelred was given bad counsel by his followers; or that he did not take the advice they gave; or that he had no follower to give advice; or simply that he was unwise. There would be some truth in all of these statements. He could never count on the obedience of many of his subjects; there were always some whose allegiance would be doubtful in case of war. It was a mixture of this and his own temperament that made him an indecisive and ineffective general. At times he was deserted by most of his followers; and the Witan elected two kings to replace him before he was dead.

Yet we have no reason to attribute his misfortunes entirely to his incapacity. A medieval king had to be feared and admired if he were to be successful; he also needed good luck. Ethelred was very unlucky: unlucky to have become king in the way he did; unlucky that the Danes should be ready for further attacks on the country within two years of his becoming king; even more unlucky in the strength and skill of the Danish leaders who attacked him. The Danes, needless to say, were taking advantage of his weakness; but the Danish armies and fleets were particularly well armed and trained and led in the last quarter of the tenth and the first quarter of the eleventh centuries. Even so, the English could have resisted them if they had been united and led by an able soldier. They were not united. Some English leaders made no secret of their contempt of Ethelred; the cult of Edward formed a centre for the expression of disrespect. Even if Ethelred had been a brilliant soldier, he could not have resisted the Danes without a greater degree of loyalty than he could command. The battle of Maldon in 991, when an English ealdorman fell heroically defending the coast in the name of King Ethelred, showed that some ealdormen were loyal; but they were not sufficient.

In these circumstances Ethelred adopted a policy which

belies his name. The Danes came to plunder; that was the basis of their way of life. If he fought them, he might lose, and a part of England would be laid waste; if he won, the Danes were bound to come again or their leaders would be impoverished or lose face. But England was still a comparatively rich country; silver was in good supply; the currency was the most highly organised in Europe. Even if England was in some disorder, the basic organs of government could be made to work; the mints could produce large quantities of highly desirable coins. If one bought off the Danes, they would sail away without committing further destruction. True, they would come again; but so long as silver was more plentiful than reliable troops, it was sound policy to use silver to protect England. And by its use, and by the use of such thegns as were loyal, Ethelred kept the country from total collapse for 30 years. For this he and his advisers deserve some credit: in counsel and in readiness he fell short of his distinguished forebears, but he kept his throne till near the very end of his life.

At length, in 1009, the Danish King Swein determined to make an end of Ethelred, and to be king of the English himself. First, he sent his best lieutenants, who raided the country with remarkable thoroughness for three years. In 1012 an immense payment of " Danegeld " was made; but before the Danes left they had treacherously murdered Ælfheah, the archbishop of Canterbury. This seems to have upset one of their leaders, Thorkell the Tall, so much that he deserted to Ethelred's side. But Thorkell's desertion brought the English king no comfort; on the contrary it brought on him a visitation from King Swein in person. In 1013 Swein landed in England at " Sandwich, and very soon after went round East Anglia into the mouth of the Humber, and so up along the Trent until he came to Gainsborough. Then Earl Uhtred and all Northumbria straightway submitted to him, and all the people of Lindsey, and then the people belonging to the Five Boroughs, and soon afterwards all the Danes to the north of Watling Street; and he was given hostages from every shire. After he realised that all the people had submitted to him, he gave orders that his host should be provisioned and supplied with horses; he then turned southward with his whole force, committing his ships and the hostages into the charge of Cnut, his son. After he crossed Watling Street, they did the greatest mischief that any host was capable of, and made their way then to Oxford, and the citizens immediately surrendered and gave hostages; and from there to Winchester where they did the same. Thence they went east to London, and a great part of his host was drowned in the Thames, because they did not bother to look for any bridge. When they came to the borough, the citizens would not submit, but held out against them with the utmost valour, because King Ethelred was inside, and Thorkell with him. Then Swein turned thence to Wallingford, and so over the Thames westward to Bath, and encamped there with his levies. Thither came Ealdorman Æthelmær and the thegns from the west, and they all submitted to Swein and gave him hostages. Having made his way thus far, he turned northward to his ships, and the whole nation accepted him as their undisputed king. Thereafter the citizens of London submitted and gave hostages, because they were afraid he would destroy them. Then Swein demanded tribute in full and supplies for his host during the winter . . . yet despite this they went harrying as often as they pleased. At this time nothing went right for this nation, neither in the south nor in the north."

In due course Ethelred abandoned the struggle and joined his queen, Emma, who had already fled to Normandy, where her brother was duke. But Swein's triumph was short-lived. On 3 February 1014 the savage old Viking suddenly died, and confusion reigned in his stead.

CHAPTER IX

CNUT AND EDWARD THE CONFESSOR

For the English throne there were now three contenders: Swein's second son, Cnut, who was not yet 20; Ethelred's son Edmund " Ironside ", who was probably in his mid-twenties; and Ethelred himself, who in spite of his long reign and many misfortunes was still under 50. At first Cnut, opposed only by Ethelred, seemed the most likely candidate; but he threw over his immediate chances by withdrawing to Denmark. It seems that he was too young, too inexperienced to deal with the situation. But he went in order to return, and was back in greater strength in 1015. Meanwhile Ethelred had been restored, but not to everyone's satisfaction; and his eldest surviving son Edmund " Ironside " was determined to make the best use he could of Cnut's absence. The details of the quarrel of father and son are somewhat obscure; but the effect was that when Cnut returned, English royal authority was divided. Edmund acted with great determination, and his path was made easier by his father's death in April 1016. But like his father he never won the undivided allegiance of the English ealdormen; some elected Edmund, more elected Cnut in April 1016. Then the two kings marched and counter-marched against each other; and for a time it seemed as if Edmund's power was growing. But in October Cnut won the battle of Ashingdon, and in November Edmund suddenly died.

From 1016 till his death in 1035, when he was aged about 40, Cnut was undisputed master of England; for most of the time he was king of Denmark too, for some of it king of Norway and lord of part of Sweden. He was the greatest figure of the northern world, and he entered into legend in his lifetime. After the emperor he was the most formidable monarch in western Europe. This was partly due to his inheritance; but also to his personal qualities, since he combined in an extraordinary way the qualities needed by a successful medieval king.

Cnut was not a man to trifle with. Before leaving England in 1014 he dispensed with the hostages his father had collected; but he mutilated them in the process. A contemporary Norse poet, singing a song with the refrain " Cnut is the foremost sovereign under heaven ", observed in passing " Cnut killed or drove away all Ethelred's sons, every one ". In the early months of his reign Cnut listened to the advice, we are told, of " the perfidious ealdorman Eadric ", who recommended that Edmund Ironside's brother and children be removed. The brother, Eadwig, was duly killed at Cnut's command, and Edmund's two small children sent into exile— according to one version, with instructions that they be slain; but this may not be true, and it was certainly not performed. Edmund's sons went to Hungary; and the two boys of Ethelred's second marriage, to Emma of Normandy, went to Normandy. Cnut was free to turn his attention to lesser fry; and in the course of the Christmas festivities the perfidious ealdorman himself was murdered in the palace by royal command, and with him " though guiltless " fell three other leading Englishmen. Shortly before, Cnut had solemnly married Ethelred's widow, Emma of Normandy. But he was a Viking, and among the Vikings monogamy had not as yet a firm hold. So he did not dismiss his " temporary wife ", as Ælfgifu of Northampton has been neatly called, but sent her into Denmark, where she ruled with him as queen. And so, in the north, Cnut was remembered as a splendid Viking: " Gracious giver of mighty gifts, you made corselets red in Norwich. You will lose your life before your courage fails. Still you pressed on, blunting swords upon weapons; they could not defend their strongholds when you attacked. The bow screamed loud. You won no less renown, driver of the leaping steed of the roller, on Thames's bank. The wolf's jaw knew this well. King bold in attack, you smote the Swedes in the place called Holy River [we have moved on to 1026], and there the she-wolf got much wolf's food. Terrible

staff of battle, you held the land against two princes, and
the raven did not go hungry there. You are swift to deal with
the race of men." Swift indeed he was; he failed in his
purpose at the Holy River, and the Viking earl whose double-
dealing had frustrated his plans was soon murdered. Cnut
had a short way with his enemies; and the result was that he
never suffered in England from the divisions and disloyalties
which marred the milder rule of Ethelred.

Cnut, then, was feared. But he was also respected and admired as a just king who ruled equitably, as a man who strove
to emphasise his position as the successor to the dynasty of
Alfred, and especially to King Edgar the peaceful, and as a
pious man who fostered the Church. We find it very difficult
now to reconcile the two Cnuts. Yet if we can try to gain
imaginative insight and sympathy into the mind of the savage
Viking who was also the Lord's anointed, we shall see in vivid
focus much that is characteristic of medieval kingship. We
cannot entirely acquit Cnut of hypocrisy. But he was a
Christian of the second generation only; his father had hardly
been a Christian at all, even in name; Cnut was brought up
in a world very unused to Christian standards. Nor could the
medieval Church exact much more than formal exercises of
piety from most monarchs. The moral standards of lay courts
were not high; medieval kings were spoilt children, and never
ceased to be. But what is striking in Cnut's case is that the
edicts issued in his name contain much more than the formal
statement of pious intentions. No doubt they were written
for him; but there is strong reason to suppose that he approved the language in which they were phrased. " King
Cnut greets in friendship ", ran a letter written in 1019 or
1020, " his archbishops and his diocesan bishops, and Earl
Thorkell and all his earls, and all his people. . . . And I
inform you that I will be a grateful lord and a faithful
observer of God's rights and just secular law. I have borne
in mind the letters and messages which Archbishop Lifing
brought me from Rome from the pope, that I should everywhere exalt God's praise and suppress wrong and establish

full security, by that power which it has pleased God to give me. . . . Now I thank Almighty God for his help and his mercy, that I have so settled the great dangers which were approaching us that we need fear no danger to us. . . . Now it is my will, that we all thank Almighty God humbly for the mercy which he has shown for our help." He goes on to establish certain rules for the maintenance of good order in Church and realm; and although English law was still very rough and ready, we may be sure that Cnut and his officers enforced some degree of law and order as it had not been enforced since the death of Edgar. To the Church he was a devoted and lavish patron; and under his rule the organs of English government steadily developed. In 1027 he went on pilgrimage to Rome, walking in the footsteps of Cædwalla and Ine and Alfred. He was able to be present at the coronation of the Emperor Conrad II by the pope; he enjoyed being received by them as a great monarch; with the emperor he could discuss the frontier of Germany and Denmark; with the emperor and other princes the rights of English traders and pilgrims on the path to Rome; with the pope he could arrange some privileges for the English clergy. But we need not doubt that his main purpose was "to pray for the remission of my sins and for the safety of the kingdoms and of the peoples which are subjected to my rule", to visit the holy apostles, Peter and Paul, and the other sacred places of Rome, and "especially have I accomplished this because I learned from wise men that the holy apostle Peter had received from the Lord great power to bind and to loose, and was the keeper of the keys of the kingdom of heaven, and I considered it very profitable diligently to seek his special favour before God ". This confirms what we should otherwise strongly suspect, that the young king listened assiduously to what his clerical advisers said to him; and especially to Wulfstan, archbishop of York, whose pen wrote many of Cnut's *Laws*, and whose mind directed Cnut's notions of English kingship. We can see a broad conception of his role emerging in Cnut's mind and acts; but monarchy still depended on fear as well as on loyalty and good government, and the Viking in Cnut never disappeared.

Nor was the element of disorder in England fully suppressed; indeed it found in Cnut's method of government new opportunities. Cnut had ruled England with the aid of a small group of leading earls, English as well as Danes. At the end of his life a great area of England was ruled by Siward of Northumbria (famous to-day for the part he plays in *Macbeth*), Leofric of Mercia and Godwin of Wessex; and his family was ruled by the two queens. These potentates were under firm control so long as Cnut lived; but his kingdoms and his family fell a prey to faction and conflict as soon as he died (1035).

He left one son by Emma, Harthacnut, who was already ruler of Denmark; but he was involved in a major conflict with Magnus of Norway, and was not free to attend to English affairs for some time after his father's death. Emma and Earl Godwin wished him none the less to succeed; but Ælfgifu and Earl Leofric, supported by most of the English thegns, arranged for Ælfgifu's son Harold (who was technically illegitimate, being son of the " temporary queen ") to be first regent, then king. There were other candidates in the surviving members of Ethelred's family; and Alfred, elder son of Ethelred by Emma, came over from Normandy soon after Cnut's death. But he was treacherously murdered; and the responsibility for his murder was fastened on Godwin—a fact which Alfred's younger brother, Edward " the Confessor ", was unlikely to forget. Meanwhile, in 1040 Harold I died, and Harthacnut succeeded to an undisputed throne. As we have seen, Harthacnut had made an arrangement with Magnus of Norway that each should succeed to the other's kingdom if the other died without an heir. Magnus and his successor, Harold Hardrada, argued that this applied to England too, and so laid claim to the whole inheritance of Cnut. But this was not accepted by Harthacnut. In 1041 he summoned Ethelred's one surviving son, Edward, to join his household, and probably designated him his heir. He was taking somewhat elaborate precautions, in view of the fact that he was probably not yet 24; but the precautions were necessary, for in June 1042 he collapsed in his cups at a wedding-banquet, and immediately died.

In Edward " the Confessor " (1042-66) we see a very different side of English kingship from that revealed by Cnut. Cnut had ruled by fear; and made his authority legitimate by removing native rivals, by marrying his predecessor's queen, by acting the part of king in every way and stressing the continuity of government; and so he won the allegiance both of the Danes and the English, and was, in a sense, the first king of a united England. Edward had all the trappings of legitimacy born in him. He was son of Ethelred, grandson of Edgar, great-great-great-grandson of Alfred. His mother had been queen both to Ethelred and to Cnut. At the same time, he had few rivals. The line of Cnut was extinct; the line of Ethelred consisted of himself and two young nephews far away in Hungary. So far as England was concerned he was undisputed king, and this gave him almost complete freedom from the danger of deposition by his own subjects. At the same time there was the threat of usurpation by the king of Norway, which rallied the English and Danes alike to their allegiance to Edward.

English kingship survived the Confessor's reign undamaged. Yet this is a tribute rather to the strength of the institution and to the historical circumstances than to Edward himself. He was a medieval king neither by temperament nor by upbringing. He had been brought up a prince in exile, without expectation of a throne; he was bred, therefore, to hunting and idleness, and these tastes stayed with him all his days. In later years he acquired a new hobby: he devoted more and more of his slender energies to the building of Westminster Abbey, and to works of piety. Piety seems to have grown on him. It is probably wrong to view him as a would-be monk. He liked to have learned men about him; above all he enjoyed the company of Lotharingian and French and Norman ecclesiastics. They reminded him of the cosmopolitan world in which he had been brought up. But there is not much to suggest that he was himself a man of learning or an intellectual. The piety of his closing years and of his bio-grapher, and the strange transformation of his posthumous career, have marked him indelibly in English legend as Edward *the Confessor*. This notion has been fostered by the story of his chastity. He was married to Earl Godwin's daughter, Edith. It is probable enough that he cared little for her in his early days; and it is certain that they were childless. But it seems likely that the story that the marriage was never consummated grew up in Edward's closing years as a part of the legend of royal piety (strange as this may seem), and as a delicate compliment to a queen who suffered from the com-mon misfortune of failing to bear children. The story first appears in the biography written at about the time of Ed-ward's death, which was intended to honour Edith as much as Edward. This biography is an exceptionally good example of the way a single source may colour the traditional view of a person. The Tudor legend of Richard III grew out of Sir Thomas More's biography, which was a brilliant historical novel, not deliberately falsified, but certainly tendentious. In the first part of Edward's *Life*, written while he was alive, his piety is already stressed, but so are his worldly interests, and he shows some notable human failings when he does things detrimental to the house of Godwin, the real heroes of the book. In the second part, written shortly after Edward's death, the author describes the king's " miracles ", and evi-dently has already conceived the idea that Edward ought to be venerated as a saint. From this developed the cult which eventually bore fruit in the canonisation of Edward in 1161. The piety stressed by the author was doubtless genuine; but it was only one stream in a personality that flowed through many channels; and if we accept the testimony written in Edward's lifetime, we must substitute in our mind's eye for Edward the Confessor Edward the huntsman.

From time to time Edward showed serious evidence of wishing to rule as well as to reign. For some years he had to submit to the tutelage of Earl Godwin, the kingmaker. But he could never forget that Godwin was responsible for his brother's murder; and he knew that in the long run his own position was more secure than Godwin's; and that Godwin could be brought to heel if the other great earls would unite against him. Edward was secure largely because there seemed to be no alternative to him save the king of Norway. By marrying Edward to his daughter, Godwin clearly hoped to arrange that his descendants would reign in England. As time passed, it became clear that this plan was going to miscarry. Edward and Edith married in 1045. By 1051 gossip was already rife, no doubt, as to who should succeed if the queen stayed childless. Godwin had perhaps already thought of his own claims, or of his sons'. Cnut had legitimised his rule by marrying the queen; might not one of Godwin's sons succeed as Edward's brother-in-law?

But the success of any such plan depended on the king, and Edward had other notions. He wished his cousin of Normandy to succeed; and he wished above all to be free of Godwin's tutelage. In 1051 he struck. Godwin was exiled; William pronounced the heir; a Norman made archbishop of Canterbury; the queen removed from court. But this success was too swift and too sweeping. In 1052 Godwin returned, and Edward was forced to receive him back to favour. The archbishop of Canterbury went into exile; the Norman courtiers were dismissed. Godwin did not live to enjoy his triumph. He died in 1053, and it seems that after his death Edward and Harold, Godwin's most eminent son, agreed to more moderate courses. Queen Edith had been restored in 1052, and in Edward's later years their relations seem to have been good. Harold never held the full extent of Godwin's power, but he and his brothers were clearly the most powerful men in England under the king. In 1055 Siward of Northumbria died and Harold's brother Tostig succeeded. One chronicler calls Harold the under-king, and in Edward's later years he led the army, and fought major campaigns in Wales. He knew how to humour the king; he organised hunting parties for his entertainment, and always deferred to his regality. He also respected the power of Leofric of Mercia.

In the mid-1050s Edward summoned his nephew and

namesake from Hungary, doubtless with a view to making him his heir. But the nephew died before he could see his uncle, under somewhat mysterious circumstances; and his own son, Edgar the Ætheling, was evidently felt to be too young to defend England against Harold Hardrada of Norway, the most famous warrior of the Viking world. For the time, it seems, Edward made no arrangement; but William of Normandy did not forget that he had once been designated heir.

CHAPTER X

THE CONQUEROR AND THE CONQUEST

The Norman dukes were Vikings by origin, and still in the late tenth and early eleventh centuries Vikings in many of their habits. Their matrimonial affairs were considerably more irregular than Cnut's; and they only practised monogamy when they happened to fall wholly under the influence of one of their mistresses. Duke Robert I (1027-35) was apparently monogamous. But he lived at a time when the normal marriage customs of western Europe were beginning to impinge on Normandy. Feudal marriage was an arranged affair, a political bargain which brought a prince or a king children, and also lands, money and enhanced prestige. This made it impossible for Duke Robert to acknowledge the lady with whom he lived; but he remained faithful to her to the end of his days. Small wonder that romantic legends gathered round this remarkable liaison. An early story tells how Robert spied Herleva at a dance and promptly fell in love with her. In the twelfth century it was said that he first saw her doing the washing in the stream which passed her father's tannery at the foot of Falaise Castle. Local legend still points out the window (which is somewhat later in construction, it must be admitted) from which Robert caught sight of her. But we may doubt if Herleva washed her own linen. Her father, William the Tanner, was evidently a substantial citizen, and he was subsequently made chamberlain to the duke; shortly after William's birth Herleva was married to a Norman baron, Herluin de Conteville, by whom she had two sons, Robert and Odo. Robert, as count of Mortain, was the most powerful of Anglo-Norman barons in the Conqueror's later years; and Odo, as bishop of Bayeux, combined the roles of Norman prelate and English earl. Odo became a brilliant, ostentatious man of the world. He endowed his diocese

lavishly, but neglected it except when driven out of England
by the disfavour of his royal brother or nephew. At the time
of his death he was engaged in pursuing the singular ambition to become pope; one can hardly imagine a more incon-
gruous successor to the prophet-reformer Gregory VII. On
the whole, and especially in his later years, the Conqueror
liked to surround himself with reforming bishops and abbots.
Odo was a survival of the warrior bishop of earlier days; it is
even possible that the author of the *Song of Roland* had him
in mind when he drew his portrait of the warrior Archbishop
Turpin. But we owe Bishop Odo unstinted gratitude on one
account: he was the patron of the Bayeux Tapestry.

William the Conquerer was the only son, perhaps the only
child, of an informal " marriage "; but as the marriage was
never made formal, he was technically illegitimate. When he
was still a small child, his father went on pilgrimage to Jerusalem (1035) and never returned. One of the wildest and
most turbulent principalities in Europe fell to the lot of a boy
of eight. William's upbringing was tough in the extreme; and
his illegitimacy added to his many difficulties. It also influenced the pattern of his own domestic life. In later years he
was to marry Matilda, daughter of the count of Flanders, a
descendant of King Alfred. The Church prohibited the marriage, but William persisted, and was in the end given dispensation. To Matilda William was a faithful husband. He was
in fact the only one of his line to have one wife acknowledged
by the Church and to be faithful to her. It is very doubtful if
it was a love-match. But its success may have been due in
part to his father's example; it may also have been due to a
desire to avoid illegitimate children: William's early difficulties, and the nickname of bastard which always clung to him,
may well have determined him to be a faithful husband. The
history of medieval marriage is like a maze, with many twist-
ing paths and unexpected corners. The Church could only
enforce its moral teaching on the great if it found allies in
their midst. If we look at William and Odo, we cannot doubt
that their mother was a remarkable woman; and it may well

have been Herleva who taught William how to be a good husband.

William's early years as duke were passed in an atmosphere of savage violence and intrigue. " The bowl and the dagger ", wrote Freeman, " soon deprived the young Prince of the support of his wisest and truest counsellors." He was protected at first by Count Alan of Brittany, Count Gilbert of Brionne and Osbern the Seneschal. Alan is said to have been poisoned, Gilbert and Osbern were murdered. Osbern was assassinated by a member of the violent house of Bellême-Montgomery, later to produce earls of Shrewsbury and Pembroke, and to be extinguished by Henry I in the last of their many rebellions. William of Montgomery attempted to kill Duke William himself, and succeeded in killing Osbern; one of Osbern's servants presently avenged his master. In the early 1040s there was a pause. The duchy was temporarily in good hands, the little duke was growing up. But it was only the calm before a storm. In 1047 he faced the most serious rebellion of his life. A group of leading nobles, especially of western Normandy, gathered round Guy of Burgundy, William's cousin, who could claim legitimate descent, in the female line, from earlier dukes. The danger was acute, but William had one notable stroke of good fortune: the French King, Henry I, came in person to his assistance. At Val-ès-Dunes near Caen the rebel army was scattered. For the first time William was able to show his skill on the field of battle. But he was still under 20, and he was still not able entirely to subdue the Norman nobility. A series of rebellions culminated in the formation of another, far larger confederacy against William in 1053.

King Henry had repented of his support of William in 1047, and wished now to crush him; he seems to have hoped to add a large slice of Normandy to the royal domain. It was not difficult to find other princes jealous of Normandy. In the mid-eleventh century northern France was full of counts and dukes enlarging their principalities; it was the age when the great French principalities were consolidated. Anjou was growing under Geoffrey Martel, " the hammer "; Blois was united, for the time being, to Champagne; Flanders, under William's father-in-law, was expanding. This process led to many rivalries. In the end Normandy was to outstrip all competitors by swallowing England; but in 1053-4 it seemed to her neighbours as if she might be conveniently dismembered. In 1054 the French king led an army into Normandy which included the contingents of Blois-Champagne, with the moral support of Anjou. The royal and ducal capitals, Paris and Rouen, both lie on the Seine; and the royal army marched in two contingents, one to the north of the river, the other to the south, towards the heart of the duchy. By the southern route went the king himself, and the duke led the Norman force which prepared to meet him. In the north the French leader was the king's brother, Odo. Odo's army marched deep into Normandy, laying the country waste as it came. The Normans bided their time, and awaited their opportunity. Presently their spies told them that the French were in the small town of Mortemer, feasting too well on the fruits of their plunder. At dawn the Normans set fire to the town and fell on the French; they achieved, so it seems, complete surprise, and the army was decisively beaten. The story is told that when Duke William heard the news, he sent a leading vassal secretly to the king's camp; and that from a tree or a rock his voice was heard proclaiming to the French the disaster at Mortemer. In any event, the disaster inspired the king with panic, or prudence, and he hastily withdrew. The story is one of many which the Normans told to illustrate the mixture of force and cunning which they felt were the special marks of their duke.

Some of William's qualities were matured and hardened early in the tough school in which he grew up. He learned to be forceful, and firm; to be ruthless, but to avoid needless violence; he learned that he could only trust the Norman barons when they feared him. Skill at arms, a taste for the hunting field, an interest in military techniques, all came young. But some of his most striking qualities and interests grew slowly to maturity. He was certainly a man of imagina-

Territories ruled by William I

Frontier not settled

ENGLAND

Welsh March

Gloucester

London

Winchester

FLANDERS

Rouen × Mortemer

Caen × Val-ès-dunes

NORMANDY

Maine

Brittany

BLOIS

Paris

ÎLE DE FRANCE

River Seine

CHAMPAGNE

ANJOU

Touraine

AQUITAINE

BURGUNDY

0   50   100
Miles

—ARTHUR BANKS

THE NORMAN EMPIRE

tion; but his ideas did not come by swift intuition. They
came slowly, by experience carefully reflected on; they bore
fruit, because William, for all his prudence, was lavishly
endowed with moral courage. His political arrangements in
England can be shown to have grown out of both English and

Norman experience, to have been a development from the in-
choate organisation of Normandy, as well as from the more
sophisticated traditions of England. One can observe his
changing outlook very clearly in his relations with the Church.
William was a pious churchman, according to his lights, and
is remembered as a keen reformer, whose activities won the
approbation of Pope Gregory VII himself. It is clear that he
always expected his bishops and abbots to be efficient servants
and counsellors to himself as well as churchmen; but there
was a marked change in the early 1050s in the kind of person
he chose for high office. His uncle Malger became archbishop
of Rouen in 1037, when William was under 10, so William
can hardly be blamed; but for the warrior bishops Geoffrey
of Coutances and Odo of Bayeux, appointed in 1049-50, he
must take responsibility; and the other Norman bishops of
this period seem all to have been worldly noblemen.

The eleventh century was an age of change and movement,
especially in the Church. In 1049 Pope Leo IX, the first pope
of the great movement of papal reform, came north of the
Alps and announced the principles of reform at the council of
Rheims. The office of bishop was to be regarded first and
foremost as a spiritual office, not that of a secular prince; it
was not to be bought; the clergy were to live up to their pro-
fession, which included (in the law of the medieval Church) a
life of celibacy; the papacy was to be the effective instrument
for enforcing the Church's laws. Among other worldly
bishops, Geoffrey of Coutances surrendered his see but was
allowed to receive it back after penance; and news of this
may have had some effect on William. But it is more likely
that it was his growing friendship with a group of ardent
churchmen which changed his outlook. In 1054-5 his unsuitable uncle was removed from Rouen and replaced by a reforming monk of cosmopolitan background called Maurilius.
Other, similar appointments followed; and even if a number of
the Conqueror's ecclesiastics, to the end of his days, were great
men of the world, the closest to him, from the 1050s on, was
the Italian scholar Lanfranc of Pavia, monk and " father of
monks ", a brilliant scholar and a fearless upholder of spiritual

standards in the Church. Lanfranc fully approved the standards of clerical behaviour and clerical reform preached by Leo IX, although he did not accept the fully developed claims of papal supremacy put forward by the papal reformers, and especially by Gregory VII (1073-85). Thus there was no inconsistency in Lanfranc taking the role, when he became archbishop of Canterbury (1070-89), which St. Dunstan had performed in the court of Edgar: he guided, advised the king, led the reformers in the Anglo-Norman Church; but governance lay still in William's hands, and Lanfranc did not dispute William's right to choose bishops and abbots, so long as he chose men who were suitable. When they first met, Lanfranc was prior of the fervent, recently founded abbey of Bec; in 1063 William made him abbot of St. Étienne, Caen, a house he had himself founded; in 1070 he made him archbishop of Canterbury. The friendship lasted beyond the grave; it was Lanfranc who put into force the Conqueror's dying wish and anointed and crowned William Rufus. Their association reveals the characters of both men. They were strong, clear-headed, masterful, loved efficiency and good order; they trusted in themselves, were born to rule. In addition Lanfranc was an Italian, a scholar, a monk, a man of sophisticated education and outlook; William was a soldier, illiterate, a man of the camp, used to hunting and burning and plundering. In their temperaments two very different worlds met in a strange, but firm alliance.

In early days this friendship had suffered a dramatic shock; Lanfranc denounced William's marriage as a sin. The duke expelled him from Normandy, and laid waste some of Bec's estates. But as he was setting out to leave the duchy, Lanfranc met the duke by accident, won a hearing from him, and was reconciled; in return he helped to plead William's cause to the pope, and eventually the pope confirmed the marriage.

The marriage was forbidden by the pope as early as 1049; it was solemnised none the less in 1053; it was eventually confirmed in 1059, on condition that husband and wife joined to found two abbeys, the " Abbaye-aux-hommes " for monks and the " Abbaye-aux-dames " for nuns, St. Étienne and La

Trinité at Caen. The two abbeys still stand, splendid monuments of their founders, at either end of the town; they even survived the devastation of the Second World War, which swept the town clear between them. But we do not know precisely why the pope forbade the marriage or exacted so heavy a price; nor do we know why William was so persistent, so loyal to his betrothed against such odds. The medieval Church forbade third cousins (and sometimes sixth) to marry, and this produced many tangles, sometimes overcome by dispensation, sometimes by defiance of authority. It was not difficult to break the law out of ignorance; nor to invoke the law to end an unwanted marriage. In the early eleventh century the French royal family were involved in a sensational difficulty on this account, and it has been alleged that it was for this reason that Henry I of France, to avoid all danger of consanguinity, married a Russian princess. So far as we know, William and Matilda were not blood relations; but the prohibition extended to certain types of affinity, that is to relationships by marriage. The tangled skein of their affinity is best avoided. What is clear is that it was not so much the technical objection as William's flagrant disobedience which incensed the papacy and Lanfranc; and it was this which made the path of reconciliation so difficult and the penance so heavy.

The marriage was celebrated in 1053. It is highly improbable that any romantic motive had led William, or his father-in-law, to take the step, although it is quite probable that real affection quickly grew between the parties and stiffened William's obstinacy in the years which followed. The whole story illustrates William's firmness: once he made up his mind, he could not be shifted. He was the most obstinate of men. But there was also policy in his marriage, as in everything he did. He needed a firm and reliable ally; and although Count Baldwin of Flanders does not seem to have given him much military aid in the 1050s, the alliance greatly strengthened the position of both parties. It was to be a vital condition of William's success in 1066. It is possible, too, that it had a closer connection with William's English ambition, since Matilda, unlike William himself, was descended from King Alfred.

When did William first think of winning the English crown? How did he come to conceive that it was a practical possibility? These are the central problems of his career. If Matilda was desirable as a princess of English royal descent, then he had conceived the idea before 1049; and there may be some truth in the stories which tell how Edward the Confessor as an exile had promised the succession to his throne to the young duke. But it is not likely that Edward himself took any such notion at all seriously; he had no strong expectation of the English throne, so far as we can tell, before 1042, and William was then 15 at the most. In 1051, however, Edward evidently took the idea very seriously. He placed a Norman in the key position as archbishop and himself designated William as his successor; and William paid his cousin a state visit. Political events in England rapidly transformed the project; the Norman influence was ousted; the house of Godwin was restored. Edward gave thought to his English relations. But it is abundantly clear that William never forgot what he regarded as his right to the English throne. He had many difficulties; France and Anjou continued to attack him; he faced the papal ban on his marriage; Edward, to all appearance, had changed his mind. In due course some of the difficulties disappeared. In 1057 Henry I's last invasion was decisively beaten at Varaville; in 1060 both Henry I and Geoffrey of Anjou died; Baldwin of Flanders became regent; in 1063 William completed the conquest of Maine. The situation in France was now extraordinarily favourable. In 1064, by a stroke of fortune still inexplicable, his chief rival for the English throne fell into his hands. Harold set sail from Chichester Harbour; the wind blew him to the coast of Ponthieu. The count of Ponthieu captured him, but surrendered him to William, who treated him as an honoured guest. The whole story is most vividly portrayed in the Bayeux Tapestry, and it culminates in the famous scene in which Harold is made to swear an oath to William on the relics of Bayeux Cathedral. This story is full of difficulties;

not least because the Tapestry in its nature does not explain the motive for Harold's embarkation nor the nature of the oath he swore. Other sources say that he was sent by Edward on embassy to William, or (more convincingly) went to rescue two relations held as hostages by William, and was blown out of course. If so, Harold acted very imprudently, or else William took excessive advantage of him. An alternative story, that he set out on a pleasure cruise, seems even more improbable. There can be little doubt that William exacted an oath that Harold would help him to the English crown; and it seems highly likely that in exacting this oath William was taking unscrupulous advantage of having Harold in his power.

It is possible, but not certain, that Edward himself still wished William to be his successor. It is clear that William had few if any other supporters among the English leaders. At the end of 1065 Harold's brother Tostig lost his earldom of Northumbria and went into exile. Athough this was a blow to the house of Godwin, it seems to have strengthened Harold's chances of the throne. England was in dangerous confusion; Harold of Norway and William of Normandy threatened it from without; King Edward was dying. It is scarcely to be wondered at that the earls and thegns felt that Harold, the under-king, must succeed; and that they over-ruled any scruples Harold may have felt and the personal feelings of the king. In January 1066 Harold succeeded, and an able warrior and an anointed king held England in a strong grip. William's chances seemed slender, definitely inferior to those of both the Harolds. Nor does even his devoted chaplain and biographer, William of Poitiers, hide the fact that many Normans thought " the enterprise too difficult, far beyond the strength of Normandy ". But William swept all difficulties aside. The Bayeux Tapestry pictures the prepara- tions for the campaign: cutting trees, making boats, gather- ing weapons. Equally vital were the preparations it does not show us: the diplomacy which left William free to desert his duchy, and gave him in addition very substantial reinforce- ments and mercenaries from many parts of northern France, in particular from Brittany and Flanders. His immense energy bore wonderful fruit: a great army was collected, with a sufficient fleet of transports; his French neighbours were quiescent, Germany and Denmark squared; the pope was prevailed on to send a banner to bless the enterprise. William went to oust a perjured usurper, to free the see of Canterbury from the intruder Stigand, condemned by successive popes for holding the archbishopric while his predecessor, the Norman removed in 1052, still lived. His leading counsellors continued to argue with him, pointing out the wealth and military and naval resources of Harold. They might as well have argued with the Matterhorn.

William's strangest ally was the weather. A contrary wind kept him in Normandy throughout the late summer of 1066, seeming to frustrate his designs. Meanwhile, Harold's resources were being steadily spent in watching the Channel for an attack. In September he was forced to disband his forces; in the same month Harold Hardrada swooped down on the Yorkshire coast, landed a large army and defeated the northern earls and the northern militia. Harold of England was drawn away from the south. On 25 September Harold and his army destroyed the Norwegians and killed Harold Hardrada and Tostig at the battle of Stamford Bridge. On 27 September the wind changed, and William was able to land his army, or at least a substantial part of it, in England. Like Agamemnon avenging the insult to Helen, so William of Poitiers tells us, he came to claim the crown that was his; like Xerxes, he built a bridge of ships which united Normandy and England. Or, if we prefer Freeman's vision of the event, the mighty Norman came to destroy the noblest of the English, " the hero and the martyr of our native freedom ". When he leapt out of his ship at Pevensey, he slipped and covered his hands with English sand or mud. " You've got a grip on the soil of England, duke," said the knight next to him, " and will soon be king."

William was king sooner than anyone could reasonably have expected. On 14 October the Norman army, marching north from Hastings, came on the English on the edge of the great

forest known as the Weald. Harold had come south with great
speed, and marched to meet William with only a small army.
It was a very rare event for a king to be killed in battle in the
eleventh or twelfth centuries. Yet Harold of Norway fell at
Stamford Bridge and Harold of England at Hastings. It is
hard to understand why Harold offered battle so soon, before
he had had time to collect his full forces; equally hard to
understand why he allowed himself to be killed. William's
strokes of fortune continued. Even so, the battle was very
hard-fought, and the campaign by no means over at its end.
The English occupied a small hill, with the forest covering
their rear, and dismounted (as was perhaps their normal
practice) to face the attack of William's archers and cavalry.
All day long the Normans mounted one attack after another.
For some hours the English front stood firm. Then the Normans, retreating from an attack, fell into confusion, and some
of the English broke ranks to attack them. The Normans
rallied and cut down their pursuers; then attacked, and twice
feigned a confused retreat, on both occasions drawing the
English to follow them. By now the English front was seriously weakened, and soon after, in another major attack,
Harold himself was killed. As the sun went down the English
fled; and although the Normans did themselves much damage
in pursuing the English down a steep slope in gathering dusk,
this sudden change of fortune could not help the beaten
English.

The English leaders were still not inclined to submit. They
thought of making Edgar the Ætheling king. William meanwhile marched slowly on London, sweeping through Sussex,
Surrey and Hertfordshire in a great figure-of-eight. He laid
the countryside waste as he went, to leave no one in any
doubt what it meant to cross him. After a few weeks, the
English leaders submitted; and on Christmas Day 1066 he
was anointed and crowned in Westminster Abbey.

The adventure was complete; and an astonishing adventure
it was. One might think that William's childhood would
have taught him caution, as it taught him to be firm and
ruthless. But as in the case of his marriage, a desperate ob-

stinacy, mingled perhaps with a kind of imaginative vision, overcame everything else. This is surprising enough; what is even more surprising is the adaptability with which he grew into the job of being king of England. We cannot pause to study this process. He conquered England, and gave the lands of the thegns who fell at Hastings or rebelled against him, and above all the personal possessions of the house of Godwin, to his Norman supporters. In 1069-70 there was a great rebellion in the midlands and the north; William put it down by the familiar methods, with much firmness and devastation. Yet more land fell into his hands. By the end of his reign all but a handful of the Saxon thegns had been replaced by Norman lords; only the greater churches remained in possession of the lands they had held in 1066. No doubt there was much rough justice, and plain injustice, in this vast rearrangement. But it was put through; and at the very end of his reign, in the Domesday Survey, he took stock of what had been achieved, what was still to be done, how England was peopled, what its manors were worth. So large, so complete a survey was unparalleled at this time. It issued in two stout volumes still preserved in the Public Record Office. The first, which covers most of England, is written in a single hand; it is probably the hand of an Englishman, grown old in the service of Edward and William. We do not know, probably never shall know, whose the hand is; but perhaps we may see in it the hand of the master mind of the enterprise, the man who worked out the detailed organisation of this elaborate and impressive scheme. He did not work alone; he had many colleagues, and ultimately the help of all the Norman barons. Above all, the energy and determination and self-confidence which the scheme reveals were William's own. He planned it at the Christmas Court at Gloucester at the end of 1085; and we can imagine the ageing king portrayed for us by William of Malmesbury, tall, immensely stout, with a fine presence, a head going bald in front, and a stern, almost ferocious expression, presiding and directing the discussion of the project. The book is a monument to him as eloquent as the Abbaye-aux-hommes. Yet it is doubtful if he ever saw it.

The main enterprise may well have been complete before he sailed for Normandy in the summer of 1086, but hardly the writing-up. King and scribe expected to meet again. But on 9 September 1087, aged about 60, the king died. In his later years his relations with his French neighbours had deteriorated. The French royal commanders had been plundering Normandy from Mantes. The Conqueror fell on Mantes and burned it; but as the flames rose his horse stumbled, and he was thrown heavily against the iron pommel of his saddle, and he received an injury from which he never recovered.

Of most great medieval kings we have a variety of conflicting portraits: their enemies reviled them, their friends flattered them. The conflicting views which surrounded, and still surround, the mercurial personality of William's younger contemporary, the Emperor Henry IV, are a dramatic example of this. But from friend and foe alike there emerges much the same portrait of William: massive, impressive, with the strength and gauntness of a great Alpine crag, and almost as inhuman. We can indeed penetrate to many human traits: his passionate desire to be king of England, his devotion to his wife, his warm alliance with Lanfranc, his love of hunting, his fondness for building large stone abbeys and castles. "But he was too relentless", wrote an English chronicler, "to care though all might hate him." Relentless he undoubtedly was; he conquered by fire and sword, and ruled by fear. He was just and discerning, and the punishments he meted out were not savage by the standards of the day, save to those who interfered with his hunting. But he was a hard man, a stark man; and although he was far more predictable, more honest, more honourable than Henry IV of Germany, Henry still has the power to bewitch us by his charm, while William still inspires us only with fear. No doubt this sense of inhuman remoteness is partly due to the accidents of time, partly to the kind of face William felt bound to present to the world. A strong ruler often makes himself appear more fearless, more granite-like, than he really is. One certainly sees a little behind the screen in the obituary notice written on him by a monk of his own Abbaye-aux-hommes. He tells of William's deathbed, of his worries about the future, his floods of tears as he prayed for divine mercy, of the immense effort needed to soften his heart against his eldest son, Robert, who had rebelled against him, how he made an inventory of his treasures and arranged their disposal to churches, to the poor, to his sons—and in particular his crown, sword and gilt and bejewelled sceptre to William, his second son; finally the author looks back over the great man's career, notes his wisdom, his inflexibility of purpose, his fearlessness. He then gives a famous description of William, which is, however, based in almost every detail on Einhard's description of Charlemagne, so that we cannot be sure how much of it was really appropriate to William. And the monk goes on to describe how William was buried in the Abbaye-aux-hommes at Caen, and how his son William raised a tomb covered with silver and gold over his grave.

Very often a man's true face is reflected in his family. The Conqueror's fidelity to his wife, and the loyalty and devotion of his second son, speak to his credit; but one is bound to say that on the whole his children present the least attractive side of him. England has had few kings as unprepossessing as William Rufus and Henry I.

CHAPTER XI

THE CONQUEROR'S SONS

On 9 September 1087 the Conqueror died, leaving three sons to dispute his inheritance. It was generally assumed that the eldest, Robert, would become duke of Normandy; the second, William, was already at the coast waiting to cross to England to seize his father's crown; the youngest, Henry, had silver but no land; yet wit and luck were in the end to make him the most powerful of the three.

The younger William, shorter than his father, but equally stout, red-faced (hence the name), with piercing eyes and stammering speech, carried with him to England a letter to Lanfranc from his father saying that William was the Conqueror's choice for the English throne. Within three weeks he had been crowned in Westminster Abbey by Archbishop Lanfranc, the primate of All Britain, his father's most trusted counsellor. The speed of his accession and the support of Lanfranc did not make his passage entirely clear; twice he had to face a major rebellion, and relations with his elder brother, who was not wholly reconciled to the loss of the better part of his father's dominions, were never easy. But Rufus had the strength and the ruthlessness of a successful monarch, and as the years passed, his grip on the throne tightened and his taste for adventure on the Continent increased. In 1096 Duke Robert went on the first Crusade, and mortgaged what was left of his duchy to King William. William's ambitions grew. In 1100 he boasted that he would spend Christmas in Poitiers. But on 2 August, while hunting in the New Forest, he was struck by an arrow, and died forthwith.

"A few of the peasants carried his corpse to the cathedral at Winchester on a horse-drawn wagon, with blood dripping from it the whole way", writes William of Malmesbury. "There in the cathedral crossing, under the tower, he was interred, in the presence of many great men, mourned by few.

Next year there followed the tower's collapse. I forbear to tell the opinions which were held on this event, lest I seem to believe in trifles—especially since it would have collapsed in any case, even if he had not been buried there, because it was badly built."

William Rufus, in popular esteem, was not the sort of man a self-respecting cathedral would wish to house. He was not popular with the Church, and he has rarely been popular with modern historians. Recently he has received more kindly, and more discerning, treatment from Professor Barlow; but commonly he has been castigated with a ferocity akin to his own. " A foul incarnation of selfishness in its most abhorrent form, the enemy of God and man " is how he appeared in Stubbs's *Constitutional History* (1873); to Dr. A. L. Poole (1951) he was " from a moral standpoint . . . probably the worst king that has occupied the throne of England ".

Rufus thus takes his place as one of the three or four villainous kings of medieval English history; and it is curious that no one so far has taken the trouble to whitewash him. Societies have sprung up to protect the precious memory of Richard III; grave doubts have been cast on the traditional view of King John; but William Rufus, though not friendless, has not caught the popular imagination—the rubble still buries him. We shall see in a moment that Rufus's character was not all black, and that his better side has been observed by a number of historians, as it was hinted at by some of his contemporaries. But the comparison with Richard III is worth a moment's thought. Popular attention has been attracted to Richard III, first by the sensational mystery surrounding the death of his nephews, and then by the discovery that some professional historians have been a little incautious in accepting the Tudor legend of the last of the Yorkists. The excitement of the detective story is enhanced by the sport of shooting at the experts. This is good fun; and in the process the experts have been forced to admit (what many of them had been saying for years in any case) that he was not as bad as he has been painted. They have also made clear that many of the mysteries surrounding Richard are mysteries still. This is not to say that he could have been a saint. No one doubts (so far as I know) that he declared his brother's children bastards and seized their throne. To his extreme defenders this merely illustrates his single-minded devotion in the pursuit of truth; to most of us it seems as vile as any of the charges which cannot be proved.

William Rufus has been brought to public notice in recent years in rather a different way. It is not alleged that he was a Christian saint, but it has been asserted that he was not a Christian at all; and Dr. Margaret Murray has argued that he adhered to an exciting underground religion of the witches, that his death was the ritual murder of the king by fellow devil-worshippers. "Walter, do thou justice, according to these things which thou hast heard." "So I will, my lord", Walter Tirel answered, took an arrow from the king, and subsequently shot him with it.

If the line of revision is different from that of Richard III, some of the ingredients of the case are nevertheless remarkably similar. Ingenious minds are attracted to Richard by the mystery of the princes in the Tower; to Rufus by the mystery of his death. The attempt to whitewash Richard involves contradicting a quantity of the evidence about his reign. The attempt to attach Rufus to an underground sect forces us to explain why this sect is never mentioned by the chroniclers— in other words it forces us to rewrite all the contemporary accounts of Rufus. There are two mysteries here, the mystery of his faith and the mystery of his death. Both are worth pursuing.

"The spirit of God takes up its abode in a human being, usually the king, who thereby becomes the giver of fertility to all his kingdom. When the divine man begins to show signs of age he is put to death lest the spirit of God should also grow old and weaken like its human container. . . . In some places the time of death was indicated by signs of approaching age, such as grey hair or loss of teeth; in other places a term of years was fixed, usually seven or nine. . . . That the sacrifice was repeatedly consummated within the historic period of our own country and of France depends upon evidence which would be accepted if it were offered in respect of an Oriental or African religion." The study of comparative religion has had its aberrations, but for my part I do not believe that its modern students accept such evidence as this.

Dr. Murray's account of Rufus's character—" a dutiful son, . . . a faithful friend, . . . recklessly courageous, lavishly openhanded . . ."—has much truth in it; and she is right to say that his savagery was of the period, that his character alone does not explain the enmity of the chroniclers. She is right, too, in attributing this enmity to his anti-clericalism, his oppression of the Church, and to his blasphemies. But her explanations of the roots of his attitude to the Church and of his death seem to me to dwell in fantasy.

A new historical theory very frequently originates in a puzzle. A scholar reading the given account of an event or course of events finds some elements in the story which worry him; the effort to resolve his perplexity leads him to revise the accepted account. If we wish to understand the roots of an original theory, we shall be well advised to look for the perplexities which started the new train of thought. The most substantial study of William II is E. A. Freeman's *Reign of William Rufus* (1882). " Freeman, having no anthropological knowledge," writes Dr. Murray, " is entirely biased by the ecclesiastical point of view, and acknowledges himself totally unable to understand the character of Rufus or to explain many of the events of his reign." It is true that an atmosphere of mystery is made to shroud some of the events of the reign, and that there is a certain hesitancy in his portrait of the king. Partly this was due to his technique of writing: he liked drama, mingled with a touch of mystery; and at the same time he never suppressed any of the evidence, however worthless, so that the sharp edges of contemporary narratives were sometimes blunted by accounts from later and even legendary sources. He was determined never to waver in the pursuit of truth; he was equally determined not to be untrue to the moral standards of his Church and his age. Stubbs was still an Oxford Professor when Freeman wrote, and his own version of Rufus was less than ten years old. They were close friends, and Freeman, a deeply sensitive man, hung on Stubbs's approbation. One suspects that Freeman felt bound to live up to his friend's denunciation; and yet he felt—as Stubbs himself had indicated—that there was a better side to William. In one respect only did Freeman go beyond the evidence. Rufus never married, and apparently had no children; and yet his private life is said to have shocked even his younger brother. This has led to the charge of homosexual vice against Rufus. There is no precise evidence in support of the charge; conditions of his age and his life make it perfectly possible. But only under special conditions would this explain the absence of children, and historians who have followed Freeman in saying " that no mistresses . . . are mentioned or hinted at " are in error. It is true that most descriptions of Rufus's private life are generalised. But they all accuse him of licence. If no children are recorded the probable explanation is either that the king could not beget children or that none grew up.

This final touch makes Freeman's Rufus a remote, untouchable man, difficult to fathom; fundamentally depraved, and yet not lacking in good qualities. He struts in a canvas from the days of Freeman's youth: dark, stormy, impenetrable. Similarly with the accident which led to Rufus's death. Freeman quite rightly saw that there is conflict in the sources; that we cannot reconstruct precisely what happened. By gathering all the rumours which floated round the event, Freeman has immensely increased the atmosphere of mystery; and in doing so, unwittingly, invited other historians to further speculation and Dr. Murray to declare that the accepted story made no sense.

The two fullest accounts name the same human agent. William of Malmesbury's version (c. 1125) goes like this. After dinner on 2 August 1100 the king rode into the New Forest with a few companions to hunt. The party split up in search of deer, and the king was left alone with Walter Tirel. As evening was drawing in, a stag passed near them, and the king shot an arrow at it, but failed to kill; it fled westward,

the king shielding his eyes to watch it disappearing into the
setting sun. Then another stag passed by, and in a flash
Walter had loosed another arrow. The arrow struck the king,
who died immediately, without a word.

Orderic Vitalis (c. 1135) tells a similar story. After recording portents, he takes the king swiftly to his doom. "He got
up, mounted his horse and sped into the wood. Count Henry
(his brother) and William de Breteuil and other great men
were there; they went into the woodland, and the huntsmen
were scattered in their various positions. The king and
Walter de Poix [i.e. Tirel] established themselves with a few
companions in the wood, and waited eagerly for the prey, with
weapons ready. Suddenly a beast ran between them; the
king jumped back from his place, and Walter let an arrow fly.
The arrow shaved the hair on the animal's back, sped on and
wounded the king standing beyond. He soon fell to the
ground, and died—*proh dolor!*—instantly."

In its main lines, both chroniclers tell the same story; and
it is clear that this was the story most widely believed,
although other versions give minor variants of it. But the
eminent Abbot Suger of St. Denis, in his *Life* of King Louis
VI of France (c. 1144), says that he had himself often heard
Walter Tirel deny that he was in the same part of the wood
as the king that day, or saw him at all during the hunt; this
denial is also mentioned as a solemn protestation by Tirel on
his deathbed in John of Salisbury's *Life of St. Anselm* (mid-
late twelfth century). John adds that many thought William
had shot the arrow himself. At the end of the twelfth century
Gerald of Wales tells a similar story of accidental shooting,
but names a different bowman. No early source attributes his
end specifically to human malice; Eadmer says that there was
dispute how he actually died—whether the arrow struck him,
or he stumbled and fell on it. The *Anglo-Saxon Chronicle*
(not later than 1121, and perhaps much earlier) says simply
that he "was killed with an arrow while hunting by one of his
men. . . . He was hated by almost all his people and abhorrent
to God. This his end testified, for he died in the midst of his
sins without repentance or any atonement for his evil deeds."

This might be taken to imply assassination; but it is plain that what his end testified in the author's mind was God's judgement; the human agent was of little consequence.

If William of Malmesbury was right in saying that the king and Walter were alone, only Walter could have told the story. Yet Walter firmly and frequently denied it. The contradiction is baffling. Regicide has always been a serious matter; but in this case one might have expected that if the common story was true, Tirel would have been tolerably happy to be (in general estimation) God's instrument in the removal of a wicked man. If it was an accident, we should be inclined to believe that Tirel was not the agent. But what if it was deliberate? We must not jump too hastily to this conclusion; no contemporary accuses Tirel of murder; accident was the official story, widely believed.

Hunting accidents have been frequent in every century, and an accident it may have been. But we have to consider two alternative possibilities, witchcraft and murder. First, let us look at Dr. Murray's remarkable version of the story. " It is clear that his death was expected, and the account of his last hour indicates that he knew his time had come. He could not sleep during the previous night, and he ordered lights to be brought into his bed-chamber and made his chamberlains enter and talk with him. . . ." Quite a saga surrounds the event. The earliest source tells us that it was known immediately (by angelic messenger) to St. Anselm in France. William of Malmesbury describes a dream the king had had that night, and then how a monk's dream was related to him: " He is a monk," said William, " monklike he dreams for money; give him a hundred shillings." And so the legend of strange portents grew.

To the modern reader all this sounds very suspicious; he wishes to rationalise, to explain. The cunning of Dr. Murray's explanation is that it does, indeed, explain the warnings and prognostications, even the king's dreams. Everybody knew he was going to die! Unfortunately, her explanation involves a number of assumptions for which there is no evidence, and which are wildly improbable.

First of all, let us see what precisely needs to be explained. The stories are told as marvels, as portents of divine grace and divine judgement: St. Anselm knew because St. Anselm was the sort of man to whom angels brought messages. William had dreams because God does not leave the victims of his judgement wholly without warning. William's death made a tremendous impression, not because of any suspicion of human foul play, nor of any suspicion of human sacrifice; but because it was seen as God's judgement on a wicked man. It made all the more impression because it was generally thought to be an accident, at the human level. In the prime of life, at the height of his power, the great man was struck down.

It is not the aura of mystery but the plain fact of the king's death which needs explaining. The stories which surrounded Rufus's death were the normal currency of the time. Similar tales grew up round other notable events in a similar fashion. Prognostications of this kind are common in the literature of the age. The legends which surround Thomas Becket's end are even more remarkable, because we know how swiftly they grew and how widely they were accepted. This parallel has not escaped Dr. Murray; Becket, too, was a divine victim. But so much has to be explained away to make a case about Becket, that it would be tedious to pursue its contortions.

The stories which surrounded Rufus's death underline the fact that men regarded his end as a divine judgement, and this is a part of the explanation for the unfavourable treatment he immediately received from the chroniclers. The Church was mainly hostile to Rufus before 1100, and with good reason.

To this hostility among ecclesiastical chroniclers there is one exception. The monks of Battle Abbey (founded by his father on the site of the battle of Hastings) remembered him as a benefactor; and it is highly probable that he put on a sound foundation endowments which his father had left somewhat precarious. A monastic chronicler was inclined to base his judgement of a king on his treatment of his own house and its revenues, and this is certainly reflected in the attitude of Eadmer, historian and biographer of St. Anselm, arch-bishop of Canterbury, and of a version of the *Anglo-Saxon Chronicle* which also comes from Canterbury. For most of his reign, on one pretext or another, Rufus was enjoying the income of the see and of the monks of Canterbury, and keep-ing the monks themselves on a shoe-string. This was charac-teristic of him. Like many feudal leaders, he regarded churches primarily as pieces of property. Anselm begged him to allow abbots to be elected to the vacant abbeys which he was " despoiling ". " What is that to you? Are the abbeys not mine?" was the king's retort.

Rufus owed his crown to the support of Archbishop Lan-franc, and we are told that he behaved himself, and kept his promises of good government, while Lanfranc lived. In 1089 Lanfranc died, and William settled down to enjoy his revenues. Lanfranc had spent a number of his best years as monk and prior of Bec; and after his death there was no one in the Anglo-Norman church of higher prestige than his friend and disciple Anselm, abbot of Bec. Anselm was one of those rare personalities who was admired and loved, even by his enemies. He was tricked into visiting England in 1092-3, even though he knew that his name was on every-one's lips as the next archbishop. Very opportunely the king fell ill, and thought he was dying. Immediately he offered Anselm the archbishopric, and pressed him very urgently to take it. He had conceived the idea that his illness was a judgement for keeping the archbishopric vacant, and would only pass if he could fill the vacant see with the saintly Anselm. Anselm had no wish for the office, nor was he super-stitious; he told the king he would recover in any case. " Do you know what you are at?" he is reported to have said to the bishops who were urging him to accept. " You plan to place an untamed bull and a feeble old sheep in the same plough under a single yoke. And what will come of it? The untameable ferocity of the bull will haul it through thorns and thickets, and so lacerate it that it will become utterly useless. . . ."

The king recovered, but kept his word to Anselm, and insisted on making him archbishop. The arrangement, however, was satisfactory to neither. The king seems to have felt that he had been tricked into the appointment, and saddled with a saint; Anselm found it impossible to keep on peaceful terms with William without impossible compromises on matters of principle. Eventually Anselm asked for leave to go to the pope for his pallium, the symbol of his office as archbishop. There were at the time two men claiming to be pope in Europe, owing to the circumstances of the dispute between Pope Gregory VII and the Emperor Henry IV in the previous decade. Officially, no pope was recognised in England, a situation evidently satisfactory to William II. From which pope, he asked, was Anselm demanding his pallium?— to which Anselm, who had been at Bec when the schism arose, and had already made his choice with the rest of the Norman church, replied " from Urban ". The king objected that he had made no decision, and that the custom of himself and his father was that no one in his realm might accept a man as pope without his permission; and whoever wished to take this prerogative from him was trying to snatch off his crown.

In the end Anselm won, and Urban was recognised; but the disputes between them grew, and when he realised that William intended to persecute him come what might, he withdrew from the country and spent the rest of the reign between the hospitality of the papal court and of the archbishop of Lyons. Rufus's excommunication was threatened, but put off at Anselm's request; then Urban died. When Rufus asked what his successor was like, he was told that in some ways he was like Anselm. With an oath the king burst out " his paparchy won't get on top of me this time; I've won my liberty and I shall do what I like." " But he did not live long to enjoy it; before a year had passed he was struck down by death. . . ."

There is sufficient in this to explain the attitude of the chroniclers, and especially of those who admired or served St. Anselm. They hated the king, but they enjoyed telling stories about him. His quick temper, his ready wit, and his characteristic oaths, " God's face! ", " By the face of Lucca " (a representation of Christ's face), made his exploits and utterances pass from mouth to mouth. We can see the picture of Rufus as a " character " growing even in Eadmer's history, the first edition of which was written not more than fifteen years after Rufus's death. Some of the stories may be apocryphal, but the picture they reveal is probably true enough. Rufus was blasphemous, grasping and avaricious; cared not a rap for the Church save when he thought he was dying; thoroughly enjoyed shocking his clerical associates—though perhaps not much more than they enjoyed retailing his depravities; in sum, an engaging scoundrel.

There is no case here for whitewash. In his dealings with the Church Rufus was violent and unscrupulous; he cannot be defended by any Christian standard. The question thus arises whether he was a Christian at all. To Dr. Murray he was a devil-worshipper, as we have seen; but her positive evidence is of the most scrappy and circumstantial kind. It is very likely that there were devil-worshippers in the eleventh century: we have evidence of various kinds of witchcraft, and the Luciferians, whose rites were described in detail in the late twelfth century, may well have existed a century earlier. But the Luciferians lived in Germany, and we have no detailed evidence of black magic or devil worship in the countries in which William Rufus spent his days. To fill this gap, Dr. Murray draws on sixteenth- and seventeenth-century evidence. It is from much later sources that she produces the evidence of doctrine and ritual on which her reconstruction is based.

Her theory, in fact, can be dismissed as fantasy; but we are still left with the problem of Rufus's beliefs. It is extremely unlikely that he was an intellectual agnostic. Under pressure of illness, he immediately tried to propitiate God. He treated God as he treated his elder brother, with disrespect, as often as he dared. Every age of faith has its blasphemers, and Rufus was an extreme example of a phenomenon probably commoner than we realise: the man who accepted the basic tenets of the Church, but with distaste; who enjoyed shrewd hits at its more intolerant, priggish or portentous aspects; who enjoyed blasphemy in open court as well as in the comparative privacy of the camp and the hunting field.

Late in his reign, William spent some time in the capital of Normandy, Rouen. Eadmer tells the story of how the Jews of Rouen bribed the king to order some of their number, who had recently been converted to Christianity, to return to their native Judaism. He tells the moving story of how one Jewish boy was converted by a vision of St. Stephen the Protomartyr. His father went to the king and offered him 60 marks (£40 in the currency of the day) if it would compel him to return to his old allegiance. The king gladly embarked on this enterprise, and summoned the boy to him. " Your father complains that you became a Christian without his licence. If so, I command you to obey his will without any prevarication and return to Judaism at once." The young man replied: " Lord king, I think you are joking." William was angry: " Would I joke with you, son of the dung? Go back and do as I say double quick, or, by the Face of Lucca, I'll have your eyes put out." The young man stood his ground, rebuked the king for his sentiments, and was thrown out of the court. The king was rewarded for his efforts with half the promised fee.

The trappings of the story are partly comic, partly repulsive. It is meant to illustrate the king's cynicism and blasphemies, and very probably does so. But it also seems to indicate something else: a sense that the Church was not always just or honourable in its treatment of the Jews. William was not an advanced free thinker, still less a student of comparative religion. But behind the cynical and blasphemous exterior lay a shrewd mind, a ready wit, even a code of some sort—to the narrow circle of his knights he was generous and honourable; and also (as he showed in his illness) a deep vein of superstition.

In the eyes of many contemporaries, the death of William Rufus was a divine judgement. This explains the portentous

atmosphere, the prodigies, some of the mystery which surrounded it. For these we need no esoteric solution. But at a
more mundane level the mystery remains: how did he die?

It is impossible to avoid altogether the suspicion that
Rufus's death was the result of a conspiracy in which his
younger brother and successor was involved. Henry was
present at the hunting expedition. As soon as he heard of his
brother's death, without waiting to see the body removed for
burial, he turned his horse's head and galloped to Winchester,
to secure the royal treasure. After a wrangle with William de
Breteuil, a leading Norman baron, who pointed out that
Henry's eldest brother was still alive, Henry was allowed to
take over the treasure, and pass on to London. To those who
objected that Robert was the rightful heir, he gave, it seems,
the specious answer that he was " born in the purple ", born
after his father had become king, and so had a better title.
This perhaps served some purpose for the moment, and he
himself seems to have believed in it; but essentially Henry
became king by strong and forceful action. William II died
on 2 August, on the 5th Henry was anointed and crowned
king in Westminster Abbey by the bishop of London—Archbishop Anselm was still in exile. By this means he established
himself as king *de facto*; he was the Lord's anointed, and
would not be easy to unseat. In November he strengthened
his title by marrying the Princess Edith or Matilda, daughter
of St. Margaret of Scotland, niece of Edgar the Ætheling, a
descendant of Alfred and Cerdic.

The speed of Henry's seizure of the throne is very striking:
it provokes the question whether all this could have been
accomplished—in particular, whether he could have been
crowned in Westminster three days after his brother died in
Hampshire—if there had been no preparation, no nucleus of
supporters formed. The question can hardly be answered;
but Henry certainly had need of haste. Rufus died in the
nick of time. In September their elder brother Robert returned from the Crusade; worse still, he brought a wife with
him, and might reasonably be expected to have a legitimate
heir. When Robert set off for the First Crusade, he made an

arrangement with Rufus whereby each was the other's heir;
of Henry no mention was made. If Robert had returned from
the First Crusade before Rufus died, he might well have succeeded to the English throne. As it was, he made a nearly
successful invasion, and retained strong support for some
years in the English kingdom. Henry might have hoped in
earlier years that his brothers would die without legitimate
heirs; but Robert's marriage seemed to make this somewhat
remote. August 1100 might well seem his last real chance of
securing the English throne; and it was singularly fortunate
that the king should die not far from Winchester. This made
it possible for Henry to seize the royal treasure and hurry
straight on to Westminster accompanied by those barons and
bishops who were prepared to support him. Is it not a strange
coincidence that Rufus died in that month, and in that part
of England?

Tirel's wife Alice was a Clare; his mother-in-law Rohesia
was a Giffard. The leading figures of the great house of
Clare, his brothers-in-law and overlords, were well patronised
by Henry; one of them was made abbot of Ely this same year;
a sister-in-law married Eudo *dapifer* (the Steward), one of
Henry's firmest friends. One of Rohesia's brothers (so it
seems) was instantly made earl of Buckingham; another of
her brothers bishop of Winchester, the richest of all the
English sees. Tirel himself immediately fled—even if not
guilty, he was clearly suspected by Rufus's devoted knights.
He did not suffer in the long run, and his family clearly
benefited from the change of king. Tirel's gains appear to
have been mainly, if not entirely, vicarious; and hardly suggest that he himself was at the heart of a conspiracy. But they
may well suggest that he was the tool of his grand relations.
Some of these family details were pointed out by J. H.
Round. They add to the circumstantial evidence suggesting
conspiracy; but they remain, as he said, circumstantial. Henry
filled many bishoprics and abbeys in and after 1100: Rufus
had made a practice of keeping them vacant and enjoying
their revenues. Henry was naturally a good patron to barons
who helped him: he needed supporters in 1100. Nor should

one make too much of relationship by marriage as a factor in politics. The English baronage had a solid core of no more than 200 " tenants-in-chief ". The Church forbade any man to marry his third (and sometimes his sixth) cousin; and although this rule was often broken, it meant that marriage among the barons was widely spread; since it was not rare for a man to have two wives or a woman three husbands, a fair proportion of the baronage would inevitably have been connected by blood or by marriage to any baron suspected of shooting the fatal arrow. It need not necessarily be surprising, therefore, that clerks or barons so connected should be among those favoured by the king. But the Clares and Giffards were favoured, and favoured early, none the less.

Six years later, after many anxieties, Henry met his elder brother Robert in pitched battle at Tinchebrai in Normandy, defeated him, took over his duchy and imprisoned him for life. A decisive battle was a rare event in this period; but even Tinchebrai could hardly have been decisive if Henry had behaved according to the normal code of the time. To imprison a great noble for life was rarely done; to imprison an elder brother almost never.

The nearest to a parallel comes from the north of Spain at the time when Henry was a child. We do not know how well informed a Norman count would be of the affairs of Christian Spain; but there are special reasons for thinking that this story would have been well known to Henry, and it is curious that it seems never to have been brought into the discussion of Henry's actions. A great part of Spain was still in Moslem hands, though the movement of reconquest was already under way. The leading Christian power was the kingdom, or " empire ", of León, which at one time or another included most of northern Spain. In 1065 Ferdinand I died, and according to custom his kingdom was divided between his three sons; Sancho took Castile, Alphonso León, Garcia Galicia. Presently the brothers fell out among themselves. In 1071 Sancho and Alphonso deposed Garcia and divided Galicia between them; in 1072 Alphonso was deposed and sent into exile to Toledo. Fortune's wheel, however, had not ceased turning, and on 7 October 1072 (when Henry was about four years old) Sancho was murdered. With the aid of his sister Urraca Alphonso was now able to return and become sole ruler of the empire; Garcia was temporarily removed to Moslem Seville. But Alphonso VI's accession was not free from difficulty. He was suspected of complicity in Sancho's murder, and made to swear an oath in solemn form by the nobles, led by the famous Rodrigo Diaz, the Cid. For this, it may be, Alphonso never forgave the Cid; their relations were never good thereafter, and the king-emperor refused to make use of the remarkable military talents of his famous subject. But Alphonso's throne was tolerably secure. To make all safe, Alphonso summoned Garcia to a conference in 1073 and then imprisoned him for life in the castle of Luna in León, where he died seventeen years later. Alphonso was free from competition by his brothers, and able to pass on an undivided domain—but he had no sons; so he passed his kingdom to his daughter, another Urraca (1109-26). Her reign was full of difficulties, but it showed that a lady could succeed to a throne.

The parallels to the career of Henry I are very striking: three brothers, one of them removed by sudden death, the other by imprisonment for life; a great inheritance united in a single hand; and a reign which ends with the inheritance being passed to a daughter. We have special reason to think that the early part of this story was known to his father. In 1072 two of the Spanish brothers competed for the hand of one of the Conqueror's daughters; a marriage was prevented by the lady's death. In 1087, at the end of the Conqueror's life, when Henry was probably in attendance on him, William was offered Galicia by messengers from rebel nobles of that province. Nothing came of the proposal, but William and Henry doubtless meditated on the story which lay behind the offer.

If Henry were privy to a conspiracy to remove William Rufus, Alphonso's story would warn him of the need for caution. Alphonso was able to swear his innocence. But when Sancho was dead, Alphonso was undoubted heir of León.

When William died, Henry's position, since he was still a younger brother, was much more doubtful; he could less afford to take risks. A breath of suspicion might have ruined his cause for ever. Spanish history contained sterner warnings of the danger of being suspected of fratricide. In 1076 Sancho of Navarre was murdered at the instigation of his brother Ramon; but Ramon did not succeed—he was rejected on account of his crime, and Navarre passed to the king of Aragon. In 1082 Ramon of Barcelona was murdered. His brother took over the government, although there was a son who could have succeeded. But he was proved guilty of complicity in Ramon's murder, was branded a fratricide, and eventually fled from Barcelona in 1096 under cover of the First Crusade.

These cases might have diverted Henry from fratricide; they would certainly make him most careful not to be found out. They show that fratricide (whether or not Henry was guilty of it) was by no means unknown among the kind of noblemen from whom William and Henry sprang.

On the whole, Henry I got a good press from the chroniclers of the day. In part this might be attributed to fear or hope of favour; in part to tact, since for example William of Malmesbury's *History* was dedicated (among other people) to Henry's most distinguished illegitimate son, Robert earl of Gloucester. But these motives cannot be applied to writers like Abbot Suger, who wrote in Paris when Henry was safely dead, and who speaks warmly of a king who had never been a friend to his patron King Louis. Nor do the chroniclers give the impression of fear or favour: several of them are frank about some of his weaknesses, all praise his virtues. God had endowed him, says Henry of Huntingdon, with the three gifts of wisdom, victory and riches; but these were offset by three vices, avarice, cruelty and lust. His insatiable quest for money was noted by several contemporaries, and has been revealed, quite starkly, from the official records of his exchequer (the Pipe Roll of 1130, the first exchequer account to survive). In this he followed the example of his father and his brother; nor was covetousness a rare " vice " among medieval kings and governments. What was striking was Henry's success in gathering and keeping treasure.

By his pious and popular first queen, Matilda, he had three children: the first died in infancy; the second, Matilda, outlived him; the third, William, died in the wreck of the White Ship in 1120. Besides these, he acknowledged upwards of twenty bastards, some, like Robert earl of Gloucester, born before his marriage, many born while he was king, of a variety of mothers. Infidelity was far from rare in the circles in which Henry moved. He was unusual only in degree; and also, perhaps, in the generosity with which he acknowledged so many of his children. For some of them he seems to have cared deeply. But he never allowed any of them to imagine that he could succeed to England and Normandy. In 1118 Matilda died; in 1120 the sole male heir followed her; within three months Henry married again, but had no further legitimate children.

Thus far the accusations of avarice and lust; what of cruelty? As king, Henry was strong and ruthless, and not averse to savage punishment. The Conqueror is said to have abolished the death penalty, in preference for blinding and mutilation and other less fatal forms of punishment. Henry employed all these means. Thieves could be hanged; in 1124, 44 of them were hanged in a day, and in the same year moneyers who issued false coin were mutilated—and in 1124-5 all the moneyers in England were mutilated without individual investigation of guilt or innocence. In later years, however, Henry became increasingly inclined, whether from avarice or humanity, to commute the more savage punishments for fines. The age was not squeamish, and Henry's agent in dealing with the moneyers was a bishop. His choice of penalties reveals, perhaps, no more than that he was particularly active, particularly unsqueamish, in meting out punishments which few seriously deplored. But the accusation of cruelty does not rest solely on these grounds. As a young man Henry had helped to suppress a revolt in Rouen, while assisting his brother Robert against his brother William. The final act came when Henry personally threw a wealthy citizen of Rouen, a leader in the revolt, from the battlements of the castle—or, as another chronicler has it, defenestrated him. On another occasion two of his granddaughters (by his illegitimate daughter Juliana) were blinded by his permission or on his orders. This was a case, quite literally, of an eye for an eye—they were hostages, being treated as their own father had treated the hostages for whom they had been exchanged—and Henry's grandchildren must have been about as numerous as the English baronage. But it is clear that Henry was capable of real cruelty.

To the modern student, Henry is perhaps the most unattractive of his family. To his father's ruthlessness he added a strain of savagery—sufficient to make him feared, though not execrated by his contemporaries. Rufus was open and generous; Henry had learned to keep his counsel, made much more show of conventional piety. Henry was sometimes generous: he bought many supporters by endowing them with baronies, and in some cases, most notably those of his son, Earl Robert, and his nephew, Count Stephen, an element of real affection seems to have entered into his generosity. He does not seem to have refused responsibility for his children. He could somehow win men's trust, for he suffered very little from rebellion; but he also won their fear, and never lost the capacity for sudden, ruthless, effective action, or the strength of mind for extreme actions. " His bodily frame was that of his family; thick-set and strongly made, of moderate height and inclining to fatness; but his black hair falling over his brow like that of Trajan, and the soft expression of his eyes, a contrast to the fierce look of Rufus, were points peculiar to himself ": so Freeman, after William of Malmesbury and Orderic. But his " soft expression " does not deceive us; we still tremble before the lion of justice more than 800 years after his death.

Henry's cruelty helps us to answer the question, was he capable of planning his brother's death? We must not underestimate the seriousness of the charge: a brother's murder, and the murder, furthermore, of his overlord. One can easily believe him capable of being privy to fratricide; less easily, perhaps, to treachery on the scale here involved. Perhaps one should allow something for the possibility that he seriously believed in his own claim to the throne. It is very hard for us to credit, but there are quite strong indications that Henry thought he and not William or Robert should be king. We are told that he based his claim against Robert on the notion that a son born when his father was king had precedence over a son born when the father was an ordinary mortal. This claim worked against William too. Like many kings whose own title was suspect, Henry was much concerned for his succession; and when all hope of a male heir failed, he tried to bind his barons by the strongest possible ties to his daughter Matilda. It is strange to us that a king who was not the obvious heir to his predecessor, whose elder brother was, indeed, still alive (Robert died in 1134), should have been so insistent on hereditary succession. His later years would have been far easier and more successful if he had settled for one of his nephews or even an illegitimate son; his heart seems to have been with them. This he refused to do; and his refusal is easier to understand if we take seriously the story that he himself claimed the throne as the eldest son " born in the purple ".

Henry did not marry till after he became king. It is true that at that time his hand was not of high value in the marriage market, but his rapid marriage to a scion of the old English line after his accession seems premeditated. The effect, at least, was that all his legitimate children were " born in the purple ", and this may have strengthened the urgency of his wish for Matilda to succeed him. One could carry this speculation further, and say: if he had a brother's murder on his conscience, how much stronger would be the urge to establish the rule of *porphyrogeniture*, which made the murder of Rufus not an act of treachery but the removal of a blaspheming usurper.

Once again we are in the land of " ifs ". The circumstantial evidence against Henry can be piled up; but of positive evidence there seems to be none. The verdict must be " nonproven ". Yet the notion of *porphyrogeniture* gives us one final, ironical twist. In 978 an elder brother had been murdered, and a younger brother succeeded, whose reign was clouded by the suspicion of his complicity in the murder. It was not a precedent likely to give Henry much joy. But there had been those who argued that the younger brother ought in any case to have been king; and in Henry's own lifetime, in Eadmer's *Life of St. Dunstan*, it was alleged that the supporters of Ethelred, the younger son, had argued that his case was superior because his father was king when he was born, that he was *porphyrogenitus*. Eadmer treated the argument with scant respect, but we may be sure that Henry, if he knew of it, did not. Like the Spanish precedent, the case of Ethelred may have warned him of the danger of fratricide, the need for concealment if one engaged in it. Ethelred may also have suggested to him a ground for believing that Henry not William was the true king. Along these lines one can reconstruct a frame of mind which might lead Henry to be accessory to murder, but there is no proof that he was. The most we can say is this: if Rufus's death in August 1100 was an accident, Henry I was an exceptionally lucky man.

CHAPTER XII

STEPHEN

Henry I died on 1 December 1135; by Christmas Stephen was installed in his place. The "lover of peace", who had inherited the Conqueror's force and guile, but few of his redeeming features, was replaced by a dashing, gallant, baronial leader, the most attractive of the Norman kings. He was in many respects Henry's antithesis; and it may be that it was this very fact which had endeared Stephen to his uncle. There is little doubt that Stephen was Henry's favourite nephew; and it is likely enough that he felt for him a warmth of affection stronger than for any of his numerous children. It was Stephen's fate to pass his life surrounded by men and women of greater force and brilliance than himself—his uncle, Henry I, his brother, Henry of Blois, bishop of Winchester, his wife, Matilda of Boulogne, and his rival, the empress. In this gallery Stephen was wrongly cast in the role of king.

To his charm and good nature even his enemies bore witness. "When he was a count", wrote William of Malmesbury, Stephen "had by his good nature and the way he jested, sat and ate in the company even of the humblest, earned an affection that can hardly be imagined." But he also implies that behind this façade Stephen was tricky and unreliable. He tells the story of how he laid an ambush for the earl of Gloucester, and when it failed, tried to laugh it off "by a genial countenance and an unsolicited confession". When he suspected treachery or was faced by rebellion, Stephen could act with great dash and bravery; but on several occasions he had his enemies suddenly arrested when they were in his court and ought to have been under his protection. Thus he arrested the bishop of Salisbury in 1139 and the earl of Chester in 1146. In both cases his own supporter, the author of the *Gesta Stephani*, ascribes the circumstances to the cunning of Stephen's supporters and implies that the situation was beyond the king's control. These are traditional excuses, but there seems in this case some justification for them. Stephen could be rash and precipitate; but his real weakness as king was that he could neither control his friends nor subdue his enemies. Events often got beyond his control. "Yet he was not broken in spirit by any man's rebellion", says William of Malmesbury, "but appeared suddenly now here, now there and always settled the business with more loss to himself than to his opponents, for after expending many great efforts in vain he would win a pretence of peace from them for a time by the gift of honours or castles." Stephen was a brave and skilful warrior; he was usually loyal and generous, if not always trustworthy; he had the knightly qualities with a touch of warmth which was lacking in the Conqueror and his sons.

He was conventionally pious, and something more. At the end of the Furness peninsula, in Lancashire north of the sands, lies the town of Barrow, a monument to the seventh duke of Devonshire and his great effort to pay his father's debts. Nestling in a little valley still just hidden from the town are the splendid ruins of the great abbey of Furness, a monument to the young Stephen, and to the feeling he shared with so many of his colleagues that the prayers of the most fervent monks available were needed to save him from the consequences of his sins. Stephen was not so sensational a benefactor to the religious as King David of Scotland (1124-1153), who founded or refounded over a dozen houses of various orders. Stephen was the founder of two. His second foundation, Faversham Abbey in Kent, was planned by himself and his wife towards the end of their lives, in imitation of Reading Abbey, which had been founded as a Benedictine abbey following Cluniac customs by Henry I, and also as a royal mausoleum; both these functions Faversham was to follow, and it reveals the conventional side of Stephen's religion to the full. Furness is more remarkable: it was first established (on a different site) in 1124, and moved to its present home in 1127. It was a daughter house of the Norman Savigny, which was already spreading in Normandy and England the new ideas of monastic seclusion and asceticism which we more commonly associate with Cîteaux and the Cistercians. The houses of the order of Savigny were taken over by the Cistercians in the late 1140s; and so Furness, not without protest, became one of the leading English Cistercian houses. It remains one of the most considerable ruins in the north-west; in early days it was the chief centre of religious life in that part of England, and had many links with Ireland and Man; and its granges and its sheep dominated the economic life of the Furness peninsula and the neighbouring fells. Stephen was an early and princely supporter of this novel fashion in the religious life.

He could afford to be generous in the 1120s. Originally indeed, he had had no English endowment. His father was count of Blois, his mother the Conqueror's daughter. But he was a younger son, and like many younger sons in the feudal world, like Henry I himself in early days, he was landless. But he was early received into the household of his royal uncle, and provided with substantial properties. The honour (or feudal complex) of Eye gave him scattered properties with a nucleus in the south-east; the honour of Lancaster gave him vast estates in the north-west, including the Furness peninsula. The county of Mortain and much land once held by the family of Bellême-Montgomery made him the richest landlord in Normandy. In 1125 Henry married him to Matilda, daughter and heiress of Eustace count of Boulogne. Matilda was a granddaughter of St. Margaret of Scotland, and so descended from the Old English kings. She brought with her the substantial county of Boulogne, and the honour of " Boulogne " in England, a very substantial group of properties which had been held by her father. Thus Stephen was by blood of the Conqueror's line, by marriage of the line of Cerdic and Alfred, and one of the two richest barons of England and Normandy. In 1127 he and Earl Robert of Gloucester, Henry's illegitimate son, disputed which of them should be the first of the lay barons (after David of Scotland) to swear allegiance to the Empress Matilda. It is clear that the two were rivals for Henry's affections; and by a crude material test one would judge Stephen the winner, since he was probably the better endowed; he had certainly won his place at court earlier than Robert.

It was perhaps out of affection for Stephen that Henry I brought Stephen's younger brother from the famous Burgundian abbey of Cluny in 1126 and placed him as abbot at Glastonbury. In 1129 he promoted him to the bishopric of Winchester, and from then until his death in 1171 Henry of Blois held both the richest of English sees and one of the richest of English abbeys. He was at once a monk and a mandarin. He was a great financier; money poured into his hands, and was as rapidly spent in restoring the finances of his two charges and of Cluny itself, and in providing himself and his churches with lavish buildings and lavish ornaments. Glastonbury remembered his keen eye for good arable land, his fondness for the waving corn. Winchester recorded his fabulous gifts: which included gospel books and crosses encrusted with jewels, vestments, frontals, curtains, carpets, "woollen cloth on which are embroidered the miracles of St. Mary", and above all the great cross, adorned with over 200 precious stones, including a large sapphire of particular value, and containing within two relics of the True Cross, and relics of the Lord's Sepulchre, of the place of his Nativity, of his Ascension, of his manger, of Mount Calvary, of his cradle, of the Blessed Virgin's hair, of her Sepulchre, of Abraham, of Isaac, of Jacob, of St. Bartholomew the Apostle, of St. Matthew the Apostle, of St. Stephen, of SS. Sergius and Bacchus, of St. George, of St. Pantaleon, of the holy winding-sheet, of the stone which served Jacob for a pillow. Henry of Blois was a man of large ideas, ambitious, grandiose, ostentatious, and yet devoted. He may have inspired his brother to become king; he certainly hoped to rule the English Church by his side. Stephen was largely dependent on him for the Church's aid in his early years, but he refused to be dominated by him. He would not have him as archbishop of Canterbury; as a compensation Henry was made papal legate, and ruled the English Church as the pope's representative from 1139 to 1143. When this lapsed, he tried to have Winchester made an archiepiscopal see, but with no success. Frustrated ambition combined with a genuine distrust of his brother's treatment of the Church made Henry's loyalty cool for a time. But as the years passed he mellowed; and in later life the brilliant prince-bishop became a revered elder statesman: no less wealthy, but more inclined to subdue his panache under the monastic habit which he never ceased to use.

Of those close to Stephen, his brother is the most exciting. Firmer in loyalty, more constant in good advice, but altogether remoter from our vision was Stephen's queen, Matilda of Boulogne. At the nadir of Stephen's fortunes, when he was imprisoned in 1141, she took over the reins of government. The two Matildas faced one another; and the irony is that the empress who had been groomed to rule England proved inferior in skill and personality to the queen whom no one had ever intended to be more than a consort. The queen's emergence was brief; but her determined loyalty to Stephen was one of the decisive factors in winning back his crown and so preparing the way for the quieter times of his later years.

The empress herself was the victim of the dynastic system into which she had been born. No career reveals the working of the system more clearly. She was born in 1102, betrothed at 8 and married at 12 to the Emperor Henry V. In 1114 she was shipped off to Germany, and was empress until her husband's death in 1125. By then she had grown accustomed to her new land, and had acquired much property there; England and her family were largely forgotten, and she had no wish to return. But she had the misfortune to be an eligible widow; and although she tried to resist her father's authority, it was a man's world, and Henry needed her for his schemes. Accustomed from her earliest years to the loftiest throne in Europe, she now found herself involved in the politics of a mere kingdom; and worse still, unequally yoked to a count considerably her junior. Matilda seems to have been endowed with some charm and considerable intelligence; at the end of her life she was able to give much good advice to her son, King Henry II, which he would have been well advised to follow. But she had been compelled too young to make what she could of a system which gave her grandeur without consulting her happiness or comfort. She had learned to enjoy being an empress, and she emerged haughty and self-centred, disinclined to control the swift temper of her family, unaccustomed to the need to conciliate her associates and subjects. Her second marriage was a miserable affair. She was married in 1128 to Geoffrey of Anjou, but soon left him. A few years later, however, they were reconciled, long enough to have three children; but they were never really happy together. In 1139 they agreed to dismember Stephen's domains: the empress was to invade England, Geoffrey to annex Normandy. This division of forces may or may not have been strategically sound; it certainly suited their domestic infelicity. Characteristically, Geoffrey succeeded, Matilda failed. She came very near to success, thanks to the skilful leadership of her half-brother Robert of Gloucester; but in her hour of triumph her temperament, spoiled by grandeur and misery, proved Stephen's strongest weapon.

Early in 1136 the English leaders had rallied to Stephen, and it seemed as if he would become master of the kingdom. The barons who had hesitated, even Robert of Gloucester, eventually came to his court. In 1137 he was secure enough to cross to Normandy and enforce his rule on the rest of Henry I's domains. But unrest was already growing. The Church discovered that Stephen was unable to live up to his promises of good government; some barons found it difficult to forget that they had sworn an oath to the empress; others found it convenient to remember their oath when they observed that Stephen lacked the effectiveness of his uncle and grandfather. Stephen was a dashing, capable soldier; but he did not have the dogged persistence necessary to subdue a ring of baronial castles, and the ultimate ruthlessness needed to make himself feared. In September 1139 the empress came to England, and a group of barons led by Robert of Gloucester made her welcome. From 1139 to 1148 she stayed in England; throughout this time she had a secure base in the west country, especially in Bristol, her half-brother's headquarters.

Matilda's arrival was well-timed. Stephen had already shown that he had none of Henry I's flair for dissipating rebellion. He tried to hold his own by rapid manoeuvres; but never carried a plan through to the finish. In 1139 he imprisoned the bishop of Salisbury, the leading figure of Henry I's administration, and his relations, and dismantled their castles. He suspected them of treachery; he doubtless thought their disgrace would be popular with the barons they had oppressed. But the only visible result was that he became embroiled with the Church, and was excommunicated by a council presided over by his own brother. While he was thus alienating the Church's leaders, who also included the most scrupulous of his followers, his weakness was also suggesting ideas to the most unscrupulous. The arrival of the empress gave them their opportunity. A baron of moderate wealth and no inhibitions called Geoffrey de Mandeville, by playing off one side against the other, built up an immense endowment of offices and land and won an earldom. Even grander was the position of the earl of Chester, who achieved a position of semi-regal independence by playing a similar game.

In 1141 Matilda found herself supported by the earl of Gloucester and the genuine Angevins,[12] by the earl of Chester and the leading turncoats, and by the bishop of Winchester. On 2 February Stephen was defeated and captured at the battle of Lincoln. For a few months it seemed as if Matilda's cause would triumph. Henry of Winchester proclaimed to a council at Winchester that " God has executed his judgement on my brother in allowing him to fall into the power of the strong "; that it was the clergy's prerogative to choose (by which he clearly meant to have the first voice in electing) and consecrate a king; and that they had decided, calling God to their aid, to choose Matilda as lady of England and Normandy. Next day the Londoners arrived to take their part in the election; but they merely requested King Stephen's release. It was already clear that a great number of people were not happy to see divine judgement in Stephen's capture

---

[12] The supporters of the empress, and later of Henry II, were called Angevins, since she was countess of Anjou.

at Lincoln. It was essential for the empress to proceed tact-
fully. Her notion of tact in this moment of opportunity was
to proceed to London, show her most arrogant face to the
Londoners and the baronial leaders, and levy a tax on the
city. Not content with this, she quarrelled with Henry of
Winchester, who rapidly revised his notions of divine judgement. The empress was expelled from London; the bishop
returned to Winchester; Stephen's queen gathered an army.
The empress was determined to win back the bishop by
force, and she hurried to Winchester and besieged the bishop
in his palace, Wolvesey Castle. Presently the queen arrived,
with a much larger army, and proceeded to besiege the
empress and cut her communications. In this remarkable
double siege it was the city which suffered most. The bishop's
troops threw firebrands from their castle, which set light to
the city; the convent of nuns near by, and Hyde Abbey outside the town, were burnt. Threatened by fire and famine
Robert of Gloucester determined to break out and get his
sister safe to the west country. This was accomplished by a
series of sorties, most of them successful—though another
convent, Wherwell Abbey in north Hampshire, was burnt in
the fighting. The empress herself escaped; but Robert of
Gloucester was captured. His loss was decisive; the Angevin
party could not exist without him. He was exchanged for
King Stephen, and with the king at liberty, Matilda's chance
of victory was gone.

Matilda's power, however, was still formidable enough to
prevent Stephen winning a complete victory. There were
sporadic outbreaks of war in many parts of the country
throughout the 'forties, though they grew weaker as time
passed. The events of 1141 left Matilda in possession of the
west country and of rather more than she had had before.
She held Oxford as an outpost of power, a fortress covering
the approaches to Bristol and Gloucester, which remained her
headquarters. As autumn turned to winter in 1142 the king
devised a plan for capturing Oxford with Matilda in it; and it
very nearly succeeded. But just before Christmas, Matilda

slipped out of the castle by night, accompanied by only three knights, and went six miles on foot, then took horse to Wallingford, through snow and ice, clad in white clothes to provide protective colouring. She soon reached the safety of the west. There she stayed, her power slowly diminishing, for five years; the king never had another chance of capturing his rival. In 1147 the earl of Gloucester died, and early in 1148 the empress retired to Normandy, which had been conquered, in the meantime, by her husband. With her departure the anarchy, which had oppressed England since her coming in 1139, finally subsided. But Stephen's hold on the English throne was still not undisputed.

In 1135 Matilda's eldest son, Henry, had been a child of two; when she left England he was a dashing young warrior of 14 or 15. He had been partly brought up in England, and given a more thorough education than most laymen received at this time. But he seems to have abandoned full-time education at about the age of 12, when he visited his father in Anjou and Normandy. In 1147, at 14, he made his first attempt on the English throne; in 1149 he made another. These were rapid and exciting adventures, with little prospect of success. But when he returned to the Continent in 1149, his father handed over to him the duchy of Normandy. The process had begun which was to convert Henry from the heir of a lost cause to one of the greatest dynasts in Europe. In 1152 the French king's marriage to the duchess of Aquitaine was annulled on the ground of consanguinity, and she immediately married Henry. In 1153 he invaded England again, in much greater strength than in 1149. Stephen fought stubbornly against him. But the Church had already prepared the way for a solution. Stephen's heir was his elder son Eustace, and he had tried to ensure Eustace's succession by having him crowned in his own lifetime. Archbishop Theobald, now in a position of effective leadership in the English Church, was always formally loyal to Stephen after 1141. But he was more concerned for the unity and peace of the kingdom than for the personal success of Stephen. It was no doubt largely his doing that the Church set its face against the coronation of Eustace, and in 1152 the pope formally forbade it. Stephen was accepted as *de facto* king; but the future was not to be mortgaged on this account. Not unnaturally, the relations between Stephen and Theobald deteriorated; but there was as yet no question of the archbishop turning traitor. In 1153, some months after Duke Henry's landing, Eustace suddenly died. This was the signal for a final offensive by the Church. Theobald of Canterbury and Henry of Winchester led a movement to bring Stephen and Henry together. They won over those leaders who wished for peace; and Henry, as duke of Normandy, had a blackmail hold over those, like the earl of Chester, who had large properties in Normandy. In November an arrangement was made that Stephen should be king until his death, that his younger son should inherit his baronies, and Henry his kingdom. On 25 October 1154 King Stephen died; on 19 December Henry II was crowned, and began to issue charters under the title " king of the English, duke of the Normans and Aquitanians and Count of the Angevins ". By conquest, luck and marriage the inheritance of four great dynasties had fallen to one man's lot. Stephen was replaced by one of the strongest, most ruthless, most imaginative of medieval kings.

Stephen's reign was an interlude between the two Henrys; under both England was a comparatively peaceful, obedient land. Why did it relapse so rapidly into anarchy after 1135? The chronicler who described the nightmare of the 19 winters of Stephen's reign exaggerated; anarchy only lasted from 1139 to 1145. In 1139 and the years which followed there was real anarchy : towns and fields were burned, castles were built without any control, and churches converted to fortresses; local feuds were freely pursued under cover of the civil war. But the anarchy never spread over the whole country, and after 1141 it gradually subsided, so that by 1145 war was an occasional rather than a normal thing. Disorder, however, was sporadic till the end; Stephen was never firmly in control. The interlude of anarchy reveals many things about medieval kingship. It shows how powerful were the forces of disorder which the other Norman kings had held in check. It shows how much kingship owed to personal loyalty. It was the tight bond between king and barons—and between the king and the people at large—which kept England normally peaceful. This bond depended on the feudal oath, on the respect which his followers had for the king, above all on their admiration of his strength and fear of his anger. To all this was added the supernatural aura of monarchy—the " divinity which doth hedge a king, rough-hew him how you will " as Mark Twain put it. But without the personal loyalty and the fear the bond was easily broken, the divinity quickly forgotten. Loyalty to Stephen was never complete. Archbishop Theobald was one of the very few great leaders who had never sworn allegiance to the empress while her father was alive. It is not entirely chance that he was almost the only one whose loyalty never wavered, except for a brief moment in 1141, and then with Stephen's permission. A disputed succession might on occasion have a chaotic effect on a kingdom. This may be obvious enough, but it helps to explain why such enormous precautions were taken to prevent it: precautions so elaborate that such an event was much rarer in English history than we should expect from the confusion of law and custom which surrounded the succession. Yet even so Stephen's failure is not entirely explained. He won the crown in 1135 as William Rufus had won it in 1087 or Henry I in 1100, while the obvious heir was alive and active. The situation was little if at all worse in 1135 than before. In what lay the difference?

The short answer is that Stephen had the qualities of Duke Robert, the unsuccessful eldest brother, not those of William and Henry. Robert's finest hour was on the First Crusade. He was not a distinguished general, but he was a brave knight and a reliable officer, trusted by his men. He had been born to too high an office. Stephen was admirably suited to be count of Mortain, count of Boulogne, lord of the honour of Lancaster, founder of Furness, a leader among the English barons. Brought up under the wing of Henry I, he had observed how men instinctively obeyed his uncle; he had also learned how oppressive his rule could be. But instinctive obedience was not automatically given to a king: he had to prove himself first. And Henry had proved himself by ruling with a heavy hand. Stephen lacked the final ruthlessness and persistence. " It was the king's custom ", wrote one of the chroniclers of the late twelfth century, Gervase of Canterbury, " to start many endeavours with vigour, but to bring few to a praiseworthy end ".

CHAPTER XIII

EPILOGUE

While the visible power of the English monarchy was threatened with eclipse under King Stephen, the ideal image of
English kingship was being boosted by the growth of two
powerful legends. In 1138 Geoffrey of Monmouth issued his
History of the Kings of Britain, whose central character is
King Arthur, and Osbert de Clare, prior of Westminster,
finished his *Life* of Edward the Confessor. Osbert's Edward
naturally bore some relation to the Edward of history, even
though the king's saintly qualities have notably increased and
the tale of his miracles has grown much longer since the first
Life was completed in or about 1066. The monks of Westminster had his relics, but they had not yet succeeded in
having him canonised. Osbert's efforts were abortive; the
pope refused the monks' petition. It was only in 1161, with
the aid of Henry II, that the monks of Westminster eventually succeeded in promoting Edward to the calendar and converting the royal bones to holy relics. This campaign was the
religious counterpart to the growing opinion that King Edward represented the tradition of Old England; that good
law must be related to the " law of King Edward " and good
kings to his family. Henry I married his great-great-niece,
Stephen his great-great-great-niece, Henry II was his great-
great-great-great-nephew. After 1161 his relics presided in
Westminster Abbey at the coronations of his successors; and
in the thirteenth century King Henry III dedicated his best
energies to re-building Edward's shrine and Edward's church,
and gave the name Edward to his eldest son.

Edward I was not likely to forget that he had been named
after the Confessor. But he seems personally to have been
more interested in his other famous predecessor Arthur; and
there is no doubt that Edward III was more Arthurian than
Edwardian. Arthur probably existed, and was a leader in the

British revival and reconquest of some large part of England about the year 500. But for centuries his legend grew slowly; and it was only in the twelfth century that he came to join Charlemagne and Alexander the Great as the supreme legendary monarchs of European literature. His fame grew up, like so many of the legends which flourished in the twelfth century, in the Celtic lands. Its early history is quite obscure. But Arthur was made respectable very largely by the daring inventions of Geoffrey of Monmouth. Geoffrey was a Breton brought up in Wales, well acquainted with Celtic lore. He also had patronage from Anglo-Norman barons and bishops, and rose at the end of his life to be bishop of St. Asaph, a diocese which proved, however, as imaginary as his *History of the Kings of Britain*. The *History* is mainly fiction; its central purpose seems to be to float legends and stories which Geoffrey delighted in as if they were sober history. But in the process he succeeded in flattering the Celts by enormously magnifying their past, and flattering the Normans by revealing Arthur as in all essentials an Anglo-Norman king. In the midst of the book are some very strange prophecies, put into the mouth of the magician Merlin. It is not clear whether these forecast a wonderful Celtic revival, or the building up of a great British empire by Norman kings to come. The ambiguity is clearly deliberate; Geoffrey rejoiced in the mystification of his readers, and in leading serious historians by the nose. There is no doubt that the English kings, in the long run, were the gainers. The chief centre of the heroic epics of the early twelfth century was the court of Charlemagne. The kings of France and Germany could both claim to be Charlemagne's heirs, and bask in his reflected glory. In the second half of the twelfth century, in the courtly romances, Charlemagne was outstripped by Arthur, and the English kings basked in their stead.

The Arthur of Geoffrey's *History* and the legends of the Round Table was a feudal overlord, who took counsel with his barons, and was condemned if he ignored their advice. In spite of this, his word was very nearly law; and it has often been observed that the tendency of the English monarchy in the twelfth century was towards despotism. This tendency was checked, and the direction reversed, in the thirteenth century. This is not to say that the barons who resisted John and Henry III created the limited, constitutional monarchy we know to-day. They had ideas of how to limit kingly power; more sophisticated notions were developed in the fourteenth century. But it was far from clear, between the fourteenth and the seventeenth centuries, that royal absolutism would not be reasserted. We have had no despots since James II, and our special brand of constitutional monarchy is something profoundly different from anything known in the Middle Ages. None the less, if it owes most of all to the traditions established between 1688 and 1901, it owes much to the divergent opinions, the controversies, the events of the four centuries which divided *Magna Carta* from the Civil War.

We cannot close a study of the English kings who reigned before the birth of John without asking what links there are between their monarchy and that of to-day. Most of the answer is implicit in the story that has been told. In the notion that a monarch is the symbol of many aspects of a people's life, in many of the trappings of monarchy, most notably in the central service of anointing and coronation, the elements of continuity are striking. The most obvious difference is that it was essential that a king in the early Middle Ages should rule as well as reign; to-day it is essential that he or she should not. In the Middle Ages institutions and customs set some limit on royal absolutism; in the twentieth century the royal office sets a limit to the republican tendency of our institutions, and performs a wholly new kind of function in relation to the Commonwealth. In these respects the institution in the early Middle Ages and to-day performs almost opposite tasks. But our kind of constitutional monarchy, or crowned republic, presupposes a long development both of representative and of monarchical institutions. Unlike Sir Robert Cotton we can no longer see the Witan as a kind of proto-Parliament. If we ask the question, from what roots did representative institutions spring in the thirteenth and fourteenth centuries, when they were born in England, as in almost every country in western Europe, the answer must be from the world of ideas and statecraft of the late twelfth and thirteenth centuries. But if we go on to ask why parliaments flourished in England more lastingly than elsewhere, a part of the answer must be that in England they grew out of institutions of local government already deeply planted. In Saxon times already royal representatives met the local communities in the shire courts and elsewhere. There was already present in germ the idea of " self-government at the king's command " which is the special character of English government in the thirteenth and fourteenth centuries. In medieval conditions, it was only possible to govern effectively if remote local communities accepted and joined willingly in the work; and so an element of self-government was necessary to strong government. Self-government at the king's command helped the English kings to rule more effectively than those of most other European countries of the day. But it also meant that it was more difficult for English kings entirely to ignore the opinions of their influential subjects.

The effects of this lay far in the future in 1154; and the deepest interest of our story must be in the way changing ideas and circumstances moulded a powerful institution—ideas both primitive and sophisticated, working in the minds of men of the most varied outlook and accomplishment; and in how the institution grew and altered in the hands of kings often of most strongly marked individuality. As time passed, the individuality was better recorded, and so we can observe with some precision the impact of Alfred, Athelstan, Cnut, and the first three Norman kings on English kingship, and of English kingship on them. But even so we are constantly tantalised by problems we cannot solve; our early kings appear before us like a row of unfinished portraits. Sometimes they seem to come to life and step out of their frames. But the moment passes, the ghosts fade back into the wall, and we are left peering at the old, worn, unfinished canvases, searching for new evidence of how the artist meant the portrait to be completed.

BIBLIOGRAPHICAL NOTE

The purpose of this note is to give some suggestions for further reading, and also to give some idea of the evidence on which the text is based. After some books two numbers, or sets of numbers are given in brackets: the first is a reference to the book, the second, *in italics*, to a page in this book which contains a quotation from it. References to books cited frequently are collected under *Sources* below.

The abbreviation *EHD* refers to the series of *English Historical Documents*, ed. D. C. Douglas.

Sir Frank Stenton's *Anglo-Saxon England* (Oxford History of England, 1943; a revised edition is expected shortly) is a great book covering most of the period. For shorter introductions see P. Hunter Blair, *An Introduction to Anglo-Saxon England* (Cambridge, 1956) and *Roman Britain and Early England* (Nelson, 1963), Christopher Brooke, *From Alfred to Henry III* (Nelson, 1961) and the relevant volumes of the Pelican History of England. Among larger books see R. H. Hodgkin, *History of the Anglo-Saxons* (2 vols., 3rd ed., Oxford, 1952), F. Barlow, *The Feudal Kingdom of England, 1042-1216* (London, 1955) and A. L. Poole, *From Domesday Book to Magna Carta* (Oxford History of England, 1951). E. A. Freeman, *History of the Norman Conquest* (6 vols., Oxford, 1867-79) is a gold-mine of detailed narrative and Victorian rhetoric. The quotations in the text (1, 113-17: *22-3*; 11, 37, 191: *153, 145*; V, 154-5: *176*) represent the more dated aspect of Freeman's book; as a guide to the sources it remains invaluable. V. H. Galbraith, *The Literacy of the Medieval English Kings* (British Academy, 1935), is a fascinating essay on one aspect of royal activity; Sigeberht of the East Angles (*c.* 631-4), Aldfrith and Ceolwulf of Northumbria, who lived in the age of Bede, and King Alfred were the only English kings known to have been literate or learned before Henry I; and even in Henry I's case the learning was apparently rudimentary and the title "Beauclerc" a gift of the fourteenth century. Stephen is not known to have been literate, although his cousin Earl Robert of Gloucester was a man of some learning and a notable patron of scholars. From Henry II's time it was normal for kings to be able to read Latin at least, and to be in some degree literate.

EHD, I, ed. D. Whitelock (London, 1955), has a large selection of documents for the period *c.* 500-1042 and a very valuable commentary on them; it contains the *Anglo-Saxon Chronicle* in full down to 1042 (also separately to 1154, London, 1961; and trans. G. N. Garmonsway, revised ed., Everyman's Library, 1960, from which my quotations are taken: pp. 60, 74-6, 106-7, 143-4, 221, 235-6: *82, 107-8, 119, 132-3, 156, 163*). Professor Whitelock's volume also contains substantial quotations from Bede's *Ecclesiastical History* (many times translated in full) and Asser's *Life of King Alfred;*[18] extracts from the earlier sections of William of Malmesbury's *Gesta Regum*[14] and Florence of Worcester's *Chronicle* (pp. 281-2, 285-6: *120-1, 135*), Norse poems dealing with Cnut (pp. 308-11: *135-6*); the *Laws* of Ine (pp. 364, 371: *90-1, 59*) and other kings; Athelstan's charters (p. 506: *118*); Cnut's letters (pp. 415-17: *136-7*); Alfred's *Boethius*[15] and *Soliloquies* (p. 844: *115-16*); Ælfric's *Homilies* (pp. 851-2: *32*); and many other sources. *EHD*, II, ed. D. C. Douglas and G. W. Greenaway, covers the period 1042-1189. In these two volumes full references to sources available in translation will be found.

Full lists of kings are given in the *Handbook of British Chronology* (ed. Sir Maurice Powicke and E. B. Fryde, 2nd ed., London, 1961), whose dates have been followed in this book with very few exceptions; genealogies and lists are given in W. G. Searle, *Anglo-Saxon Bishops, Kings and Nobles* (Cambridge, 1899), which is elderly but still very useful.

---

[18] Also translated in full by J. A. Giles, *Six Old English Chronicles* (London, 1882). My quotations from Bede and Asser are my own translations: from *Historia Ecclesiastica*, i, 15, ii, 9-14, iii, 25: pp. *86, 95, 98*; *Asser's Life of King Alfred*, ed. W. M. Stevenson (Oxford, 1904), pp. 2 ff.: *75*; 73ff.: *111-12*; 76 ff.: *105-6*; 136 (Chron. St. Neot's): *108-9*.

[14] The quotations on pp. *153, 158-9* are my own translation from *Gesta Regum*, ed. W. Stubbs (Rolls Series), II (1889), 300, 378-9.

[15] Pp. 845-6; *114-15*; I have italicised the words which bear some relation to what Boethius wrote. This passage contains one of the longest digressions in the Boethius; the digressions are often much longer in the Orosius, and in the *Soliloquies* Alfred sat quite free to his original.

Chapter I

Yeavering will be the subject of a forthcoming book by B. Hope-Taylor; Sutton Hoo is discussed by R. L. S. Bruce-Mitford in *The Sutton Hoo Ship Burial, a provisional guide* (British Museum, 5th impression, 1956; also in an appendix to Hodgkin, above);[16] the best reproduction of the Bayeux Tapestry is in the Phaidon Press edition (2nd ed., 1965), with commentary by Sir Frank Stenton, F. Wormald and others; for coins see G. C. Brooke, *English Coins* (revised ed., London, 1950), and (more specialised), *Anglo-Saxon Coins*, ed. R. H. M. Dolley (London, 1961).

Chapters II and III

The problems discussed in Chapters II and III are dealt with in some measure in the general books listed above.[17] The best account of Anglo-Saxon king-making is in H. M. Chadwick, *Studies in Anglo-Saxon Institutions* (Cambridge, 1905), pp. 292 ff., 357 ff., to which my text owes much. Most earlier and some more recent writers have tended to make too much, or too imprecise use of the word " election "; this is partly explained in the text, but is also partly due to the language of the Norman chroniclers. Thus

---

[16] On the date of Sutton Hoo see P. Grierson, *Antiquity*, XXVI (1952), 83-6. S. Lindqvist, " Skeppsgraven å Sutton Hoo ", *Kungl. Humanistika Vetenskaps samfundet i Uppsala, Årsbok 1951*, pp. 77 ff. (I owe this reference to Mr. J. V. H. Eames), suggests, *inter alia*, that the large dish contained the ashes of Æthelhere, cremated, perhaps by the Winwæd, so that the grave is not, in his view, entirely empty. He also works out in detail the connection of the armour with Sweden. For an interesting recent discussion see J. M. Wallace-Hadrill in *Studi medievali*, 3rd ser., I, i (Spoleto, 1960), 177-94, who suggests that it is doubtful if the burial is royal—that the question should at present be left open. (See now Mrs. S. Glass in *Antiquity*, XXXVI (1962), 179-83, who argues for a date in the 640s. The debate continues.) (See p. 203)

[17] For a general survey of German kingship, see F. Kern, *Kingship and Law in the Middle Ages* (Oxford, 1939); on king-making in the early Middle Ages, P. Grierson, *Cambridge Historical Journal*, VII, 1-22 (1941); and the development of " elections " in Germany, H. Mitteis, *Die deutsche Königswahl* (Brünn, 1944), which is fundamental for our understanding of the process of designation.

William of Malmesbury makes Harold claim the crown because he was chosen by the English " senate ". (For an interesting study of the Witan see F. Liebermann, *The National Assembly in the Anglo-Saxon Period* (Halle, 1913)). The quotation from Ælfric (cited Chadwick, p. 357 n.; translater *EHD*, I, 851-2) also suggests that some ecclesiastics had a larger view of the nature of election than most laymen; we must make allowance for diversity of views; but essentially William is indulging in the fashion for clothing contemporary institutions in classical dress, and Ælfric may have stretched the notion of choice to fit the analogy of sin, which he is working out. It is improbable that the analogy was meant to be pressed. The argument that Ethelred II claimed the throne because his father was king when he was born is given by Eadmer in his life of St. Dunstan (W. Stubbs, *Memorials of St. Dunstan*, Rolls Series, 1874, p. 214). It is not in any of Eadmer's known sources.

On the coronation see P. E. Schramm, *A History of the English Coronation* (Oxford, 1937); the early rites are printed by Professor Schramm in *Zeitschrift der Savigny-Stiftung für Rechtsgeschichte*, Kanonistische Abteilung XXIII (1935) (pp. 222 ff.; 231 ff.: 36-8); on the crown and other regalia see Schramm, *Herrschaftszeichen und Staatssymbolik* (3 vols., Stuttgart, 1954-6); M. R. Holmes, " The Crowns of England ", *Archaeologia*, LXXXVI (1936), 73-90.

For the literature on the succession to Edward the Confessor, see *The Life of King Edward the Confessor*, ed. F. Barlow (Nelson's Medieval Texts, 1962), p. 79 and n., cf. p. lxv n., and above *figures 9f, 10a;*[18] and on the accession of Stephen, Freeman, *Norman Conquest*, v, 856 ff.; J. H. Round, *Geoffrey de Mandeville* (London, 1892), chapter I (and below).[19]

For most of the sources used here, see above. *Beowulf* has been many times translated: I have quoted from the version by D.

---

[18] Barlow, pp. 40-52, 60 are quoted on pp. *62-4*; cf. p. 60 n. 5. A revised version of the events of 1051 is proposed by D. C. Douglas, *English Historical Review*, LXVIII (1953), 526 ff.

[19] But my interpretation differs substantially from those of Freeman and Round. Round's view that the case was discussed before the pope in 1136 has been disproved by R. L. Poole in his edition of John and Salisbury's *Historia Pontificalis* (Oxford, 1927), appendix VI, who placed the discussion in the Lateran Council of 1139. My quotation from John is from Mrs. M. Chibnall's edition (Nelson's Medieval Texts, 1956, pp. 84-5); Gilbert Foliot's letter is no. 26 in the edition of Z. N. and C. N. L. Brooke and A. Morey. For the claim of the citizens of London see M. McKisack in *Studies in Medieval History Presented to F. M. Powicke* (Oxford, 1948), pp. 76 ff.

Wright (Penguin Classics, 1957: pp. 27-8, 28-9: *51, 56-7; 35: 58; 50, 56: 67; 61: 65; 76-7: 57; 79: 59*); among contemporaries, see especially D. Whitelock, *The Audience of Beowulf* (Oxford, 1951). For Norman castles see R. A. Brown, *English Medieval Castles* (Batsford, 1954), and for early Norman costumes and armour, *The Bayeux Tapestry*. On the "Anonymous of York", see G. H. Williams, *The Norman Anonymous of 1100 A.D.* (Harvard, 1951). The list of Henry I's household is printed in *Dialogus de Scaccario*, ed. C. Johnson (Nelson's Medieval Texts, 1950), pp. 128-35; on royal government see especially V. H. Galbraith, *Studies in the Public Records* (Edinburgh, 1948), chapter 2.

Chapters IV and V

Genealogical tables are worked out in Searle (above), and discussed (among many others) by R. W. Chambers, *Beowulf, an Introduction* (3rd ed., Cambridge, 1959), in a very interesting way; but study of them has been put on a new foundation by K. Sisam, "Anglo-Saxon Royal Genealogies", *Proceedings of the British Academy*, XXXIX (1953), 287-348.[20] Sir Frank Stenton's study of the kings of Lindsey is in *Essays in History presented to R. L. Poole* (Oxford, 1927), pp. 136-50. The problems of using genealogies as historical evidence are well illustrated in E. Peters's article in the *Journal of the Royal Anthropological Institute*, XC (1960), 29-53. The title *Bretwalda* has been most recently discussed by Mrs. N. K. Chadwick in *Bulletin of the Board of Celtic Studies*, XIX (Cardiff, 1961), 225-30. For sources, see above; *Widsith* is quoted from R. K. Gordon, *Anglo-Saxon Poetry* (Everyman Library, revised ed., 1954), p. 68.

The history of the early settlements and the early kingdoms is both obscure and controversial, and it is impossible to do justice to the controversies in a book of this character. For an expert summary of recent views, see P. Hunter Blair, *Introduction to Anglo-Saxon England* and *Roman Britain and Early England*; for an example of a case history, see his *Origins of Northumbria* (Gateshead, 1948). My account of the nomenclature of the kingdoms owes much to H. E. Walker, "Bede and the Gewissae", *Cambridge*

---

[20] In the genealogy on p. 75 I have quoted the original text of Asser following Mr. Sisam's spellings, save for the biblical characters; in the earlier parts of the genealogies on pp. 206-9 I have also followed Mr. Sisam where possible, and otherwise adopted the spelling of the Vespasian lists printed by H. Sweet, *Oldest English Texts* (Early English Text Soc., 1885), pp. 169 ff.

Historical Journal, XII, 174-86 (1956); cf. (on "Northumbria"), J. N. L. Myres, *History*, XX (1935-6), 250-62. On the general background of ideas of early kingship, see H. M. Chadwick, *The Heroic Age* (Cambridge, 1912).

Chapter VI

The reign of Offa is a remarkable example of an important phase in English history which has to be reconstructed by detective work on charters and monuments. Offa's charters make grants of land in many different parts of the country, and so reveal the development and spread of his power; they confirm acts of and are witnessed by other kings, sub-kings and ealdormen, and so reveal the way in which he reduced some kings to ealdormen, and exercised authority over others. Offa's title in the charters also reveals his rise to the position of *Bretwalda*—from *rex Merciorum* (kings of the Mercians), via *rex Anglorum*, to *rex totius Anglorum patriae* (king of the whole country of the English. This has been worked out by Sir Frank Stenton in " The Supremacy of the Mercian Kings ", *English Historical Review*, XXXIII (1918), 433-52 (summarised in *Anglo-Saxon England*, pp. 205 ff.). In an equally striking way, Offa's power is revealed by his dyke, whose history is brilliantly reconstructed in Sir Cyril Fox's *Offa's Dyke* (London, 1955), which contains a detailed survey both of Offa's and Wat's dykes.

Chapter VII

On Alfred, see *Asser's Life*, and Eleanor Duckett, *Alfred the Great and his England* (London, 1957). For his works, see translations of the *Pastoral Care* and Orosius, Boethius and *Soliloquies* by H. Sweet (Early English Text Society, 1871 and 1883), W. J. Sedgefield (Oxford, 1900) and H. L. Hargrove, *Yale Studies in English*, XXII (1904); also by S. Potter, *Philologus*, XCVIII (1949); extracts in *EHD*, I—see above. On Alfred's methods see K. Sisam, *Studies in the History of Old English Literature* (Oxford, 1953), pp. 140-7. The *Chronicle of St. Neot's* was analysed with an elaborate commentary in W. H. Stevenson's edition of Asser (on the legend of the cakes see pp. 136, 256 ff.).

Chapter VIII

On Athelstan as a collector of books and relics, see J. Armitage Robinson, *The Times of St. Dunstan* (Oxford, 1923) (pp. 60, 73,

80: *120, 123-4*; other sources from *EHD*, I, see above); on Edgar
as a patron of the monastic revival, see *Regularis Concordia*, ed.
T. Symons (Nelson's Medieval Texts, 1953) (pp. 1-2: *127-8*), Eric
John, " The King and the Monks in the Tenth-Century Reformation ", *Bulletin of the John Rylands Library*, XLII (1959-60), 61-87,
and T. Symons, in *Downside Review*, LXXX (1962), 55 ff., 140 ff.;
and on the revival in general, D. Knowles, *The Monastic Order in
England* (Cambridge, 1940). On the succession of Ethelred, see
EHD, I, 841-3 (from the *Life of St. Oswald*), and above.

Chapter IX

On Cnut see L. M. Larson, *Canute the Great* (New York, 1912); on
Edward the Confessor, the *Life*, ed. F. Barlow.

Chapters X and XI

Here Freeman's *Norman Conquest* and *Reign of William Rufus*
(2 vols., Oxford, 1882) (II, 502-3: *162*) still provide the fullest
narrative, and his appendices give a full account of the sources
(especially, *Norman Conquest*, II (2nd ed.), U-X on William's early
life; III (2nd ed.), O on his marriage; *William Rufus*, II, G, SS for
Rufus's character and death; *Norman Conquest*, IV, EE on Henry
I's birth, V, X for his character). Sir Frank Stenton's *William the
Conqueror* (London, 1908) is the standard modern biography; on
William II see especially Barlow, *Feudal Kingdom*, pp. 147-70; my
quotations from Stubbs and A. L. Poole are from *Constitutional
History*, I (1874), 328 (*159*) and *From Domesday Book to Magna
Carta*, p. 99 (*159*). Dr. Margaret Murray's theories were pro-
pounded in *The God of the Witches* (London, 1931, pp. 160-1, 162,
165, 167-8: *160* ff.). J. H. Round's study of the relations of
Walter Tirel is in *Feudal England* (London, 1895), pp. 468 ff. (the
book which also contains Round's famous studies on the battle of
Hastings; and on Domesday Book, for which see V. H. Galbraith,
The Making of Domesday Book (Oxford, 1961)). For the Spanish
events described in this chapter see R. Menéndez Pidal, *The Cid
and his Spain* (Eng. trans. London, 1934), especially pp. 115 ff.,
133; for the betrothal of the Conqueror's daughter, Freeman,
Norman Conquest, IV, appendix TT and William of Poitiers, *Gesta
Guillelmi*, ed. R. Foreville (Paris, 1952), p. 143 and note. The most
important narrative of William II's death not referred to in the text
is probably that of Geoffrey Gaimar, written in the late 1130s,
which implies at one moment that Tirel was in a conspiracy, but
still makes the death an accident; there is no space here to enter into

the problems raised by this account, which has certainly some
fiction in it. (Ed. A. Bell, Oxford, 1960, pp. 198 ff.).

For the Conqueror, especially valuable sources are the *Bayeux
Tapestry*, William of Poitiers, William of Malmesbury, the obituary
notices of the *Anglo-Saxon Chronicle* and the monk of Caen (p.
157 is based on T. D. Hardy, *Descriptive Catalogue of Materials
Relating to the History of Great Britain and Ireland*, Rolls
Series, II (1865), 14-15 note; see also *EHD*, II, 279-80), and
Orderic Vitalis. The chief sources for Rufus's death are Orderic
(ed. A. Le Prevost and L. Delisle, 5 vols., Paris, 1838-55) (IV, 86-7:
163; my own translation; p. *160* from Margaret Murray, p. *168*;
Orderic is being translated by M. Chibnall (Oxford, 1968-   ),
William of Malmesbury, Eadmer (*Historia Novorum*, ed. M. Rule,
Rolls Series, 1884 (now translated by G. Bosanquet, London,
1964), pp. 36 49, 100-1, 116: *166-7*), and Suger (*Vie de Louis VI
le Gros*, ed. and trans. H. Waquet, Paris, 1929, see p. 12). John of
Salisbury's *Life of Anselm* is in Migne, *Patrolog. Latina*, CXCIX (see
col. 1031).

Chapter XII

The chief sources for Stephen's reign are the *Historia Novella* of
William of Malmesbury and the *Gesta Stephani* (both ed. K.
Potter, Nelson's Medieval Texts, 1955); on the *Gesta* see above, p.
45 n. (*Historia Novella*, pp. 18, 21-3: *179-80*; 53: *185*). On his
reign see especially J. H. Round, *Geoffrey de Mandeville* (London,
1892); Stenton, *First Century of English Feudalism* (revised ed.,
Oxford, 1962); on Henry of Blois, Knowles, *Monastic Order*,
chapter xvi (repr. in *Saints and Scholars*, Cambridge, 1962), L.
Voss, *Heinrich von Blois* (Berlin, 1932), and for his gifts to Winchester Cathedral, E. Bishop, *Liturgica Historica* (Oxford, 1918),
pp. 392-401.

Chapter XIII

Geoffrey of Monmouth's *History* was translated by J. A. Giles (*Six
Old English Chronicles*); for the cult of Edward the Confessor, see
Life, ed. Barlow, appendix D.

ADDITIONAL NOTE (1971)

On two topics in particular there has been intensive research since 1963: on Sutton Hoo and on the Norman Conquest. The finds at Sutton Hoo have been re-examined and the site re-excavated, and the numismatic evidence has been reappraised. It now seems much more likely that the burial belongs to the 620s, and that it was Raedwald's; the whetstone looks more like a sceptre, but the helmet has changed its shape entirely. We still await final publication, and with even greater impatience the excavation of the other mounds, for substantial finds in at least two now seem probable. Under these circumstances it would be premature to revise my text; but it is essential to draw attention to these exciting discoveries and even more exciting possibilities.

1966 brought a spate of books and articles on 1066, which re-opened many old problems. Perhaps the most doubtful opinions stated above are now those which relate to William I's claim to the English throne: a more complex hereditary claim seems likely, and any *formal* designation by Edward the Confessor much less so. On all this see the discussions in Guy of Amiens, *Carmen de Hastingae Proelio*, ed. C. Morton and H. Muntz (Oxford Medieval Texts, forthcoming). Of the reinterpretations of the Conquest, D. Matthew, *The Norman Conquest* (London, 1966), is especially interesting.

Recent Literature

A very important recent study is J. M. Wallace-Hadrill, *Early Germanic Kingship in England and on the Continent* (Oxford, 1971); see also D. A. Binchy, *Celtic and Anglo-Saxon Kingship* (Oxford, 1970); W. A. Chaney, *The Cult of Kingship in Anglo-Saxon England* (Manchester, 1970).

On the Anglo-Saxons, their life and art, see D. M. Wilson, *The Anglo-Saxons* (London, 1960); on the Vikings, P. Sawyer, *The Age of the Vikings* (London, 1962) and P. G. Foote and D. M. Wilson, *The Viking Achievement* (London, 1970); on Yeavering and Cheddar, *The History of the King's Works*, ed. H. M. Colvin, I (London, 1963), 1ff.

On the kings from 1042 to 1154, see F. Barlow, *Edward the Confessor* (London, 1970); D. C. Douglas, *William the Conqueror* (London, 1964); R. W. Southern, ' The place of Henry I in English history', *Proceedings of the British Academy*, 1962, reprinted in *Medieval Humanism and Other Studies* (Oxford, 1970), chap. 11; see also, Southern, *St. Anselm and His Biographer* (Cambridge, 1963); R. H. C. Davis, *King Stephen* (London, 1967); H. A. Cronne, *The Reign of Stephen* (London, 1970).

Professor V. H. Galbraith has published his doubts on Asser's authenticity in his *Introduction to the Study of History* (London, 1964); see D. Whitelock, *The Genuine Asser* (Reading, 1968). The argument on Matilda's case before the pope has been reinterpreted in A. Morey and C. N. L. Brooke, *Gilbert Foliot and his Letters* (Cambridge, 1965), chap. VII.

GENEALOGICAL TABLES

The following are simplified versions of the genealogies of the kings of Northumbria, Mercia, Wessex and England. Full lists of kings are given in the *Handbook of British Chronology*, ed. F. M. Powicke and E. B. Fryde (2nd ed., London, 1961), and genealogies in W. G. Searle, *Anglo-Saxon Bishops, Kings and Nobles* (Cambridge, 1899; cf. above, p. 199). The early names on these genealogies may well be at least partly fictitious; the information becomes more reliable as the centuries pass. Often in early times a family group reigned simultaneously; this tends to be hidden in these tables: it is not possible to give all the known colleagues without making the tables wholly unintelligible. Many younger brothers and cadet branches are not shown.

Names in capital letters are mentioned in the text of the book. Those with dates were certainly kings (etc.); of those without dates some probably held kingly rank, many may have done, some certainly did not.

In a forthcoming article[21] my colleague Dr. David Kirby is proposing a revision of Bede's chronology which would alter the dates of many of the sixth- and seventh-century kings. It seems best to leave the conventional dates in this book, since his revision has not yet been published or considered by other experts.

[21] Now in *English Historical Review*, LXXVIII (1963); see also Kirby, ibid., LXXX (1965), for the early West Saxon kings.

1 NORTHUMBRIA (down to 729)

DEIRA

BERNICIA
(After 593—or perhaps a little earlier—the kingdoms were usually under one king)

WODEN

DEIRA
- Wegdæg
- Siggar
- Swæbdæg
- Siggeot
- Sæbald
- Sæfugul
- Soemel
- Uestorualcna
- Uilgils
- Uuscfrea

BERNICIA
- Baldæg
- Bernic
- Wegbrand
- Ingibrand
- Alusa
- Angengeot
- Æthelbert
- Oesa
- Eoppa
- Ida
  (c. 547–c. 560)

Yffi

Ælle
(c. 560–90)

EDWIN
(616–34)

Ælfric

Osric
(632–3)

Oswine
(644–51)

Ethelwald
(651–4)

Ada

Ethelric

Theodric

Ethelfrith
(593–616)

Eanfrith
(632–3)

St. Oswald
(633–41)

Oswiu
(641–70)

Egfrith
(670–85)

Aldfrith
(685–704)

Osred I
(705–16)

Osric
(718–29)

(The kingdom passed to other families in the course of the early eighth century, but survived until about 878, when it was conquered by the Vikings, who set up a kingdom based on York which lasted until the mid-tenth century.)

3 MERCIA

WODEN — Watholgeot — Uihtlæg — Uermund — OFFA — Angengeot — Eamer — Icil — Cnebba — Cynewald — Crioda — Pypba —

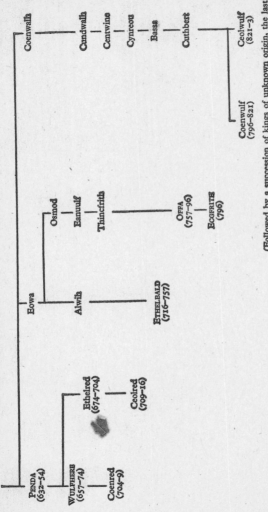

Penda (632–54) ─┬─ Wulfhere (657–74) ── Coenred (704–9)
                │
                └─ Ethelred (674–704) ── Ceolred (709–16)

Eowa ─┬─ Osmod ─┬─ Eanulf
      │   └─ Thincfrith ── Offa (757–96) ── Ecgfrith (796)
      │
      └─ Alwih ── Ethelbald (716–757)

Coenwalh ─┬─ Cundwalh
          ├─ Centwine
          ├─ Cynreou
          ├─ Bassa
          └─ Cuthbert ─┬─ Coenwulf (796–821) ── Ceolwulf (821–3)

(Followed by a succession of kings of unknown origin, the last of whom, Burgred, was replaced by the ealdorman Ethelred before 883)

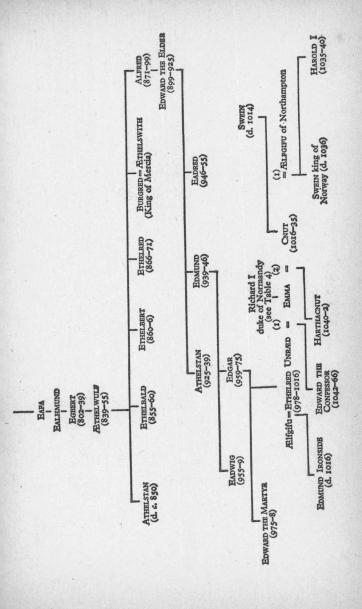

4 THE NORMAN KINGS

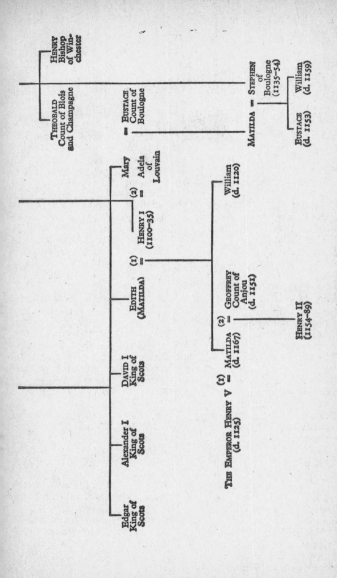

INDEX

Numbers in italic type refer to the Illustrations

214